The State
of
Church Giving
through 1997

www.emptytomb.org

**Ninth Edition**

# The State
# of
# Church Giving
# through 1997

John L. Ronsvalle

Sylvia Ronsvalle

*empty tomb, inc.*
Champaign, Illinois

*The State of Church Giving through 1997*
by John and Sylvia Ronsvalle
published by empty tomb, inc.
First printing, December 1999
Second printing, January 2000

empty tomb, inc.
301 N. Fourth Street
P.O. Box 2404
Champaign, IL 61825-2404
Phone: (217) 356-9519
Fax: (217) 356-2344
www.emptytomb.org

ISBN 0-9639962-9-0
ISSN 1097-3192

The Library of Congress has catalogued this publication
as follows:
The state of church giving through ...—19uu- Champaign, Ill. :
Empty Tomb, Inc.,
v. : ill. ; 28 cm. Annual.
1. Christian giving Periodicals.
2. Christian giving Statistics Periodicals.
3. Church finance—United States Periodicals.
4. Church finance—United States Statistics Periodicals.
    BV772 .S32 98-640917

# CONTENTS

# TABLES AND FIGURES

# PREFACE

History can slip through your fingers. Taking the time today to preserve information that will be important tomorrow is a critically important activity. Even so, in the press of many other demands, recording and reporting denominational data can seem like "extra" work. Yet, through the rich tradition of church officials reporting to the *Yearbook of American and Canadian Churches* (YACC) series, researchers today can obtain a view of giving throughout this century.

We therefore want to express a deep sense of appreciation to the church officials in different communions who extend this data set by continuing to report information in an ongoing basis. Their role in preserving history, and providing numbers that can help guide decisions for the future as well, is a vital one.

Since 1916, yearbook staff have processed and published records from many communions in a single annual volume, making the information available to the general public, church leaders, and academics alike. For many years now, this activity has found a home in the National Council of the Churches of Christ in the U.S.A. (NCC). Credit goes to the leadership of Joan B. Campbell, NCC General Secretary, for preserving this evolving data source.

Eileen Lindner, the NCC Associate General Secretary for Christian Unity, now also serves as *YACC* editor. She has brought an appreciation of the *YACC*'s historical contribution and a breadth of commitment to the church in the U.S. that has already served to strengthen this series. It has been our pleasure to work with her, and Derek Lander, her assistant, in relationship to the data collection and preservation.

We would like to thank Sarah Sung Yoon Hartmann, our administrative assistant. She has not only contributed her many talents to the production of this volume, but she has been a friend in the process. The assistance of Linda Kennedy has also been a valuable resource as we completed the presentation of this work.

The goal is to provide accurate information that provides the reader with a basis for evaluating church giving patterns. It is our hope that a fresh look at the facts will contribute to church members fulfilling more of our common potential for loving a hurting world in Jesus' name.

John L. Ronsvalle, Ph.D.
Sylvia Ronsvalle

Champaign, Illinois
November 1999

# SUMMARY_____

*The State of Church Giving through 1997* is the most recent report in a series that considers denominational giving data for a set of denominations first analyzed in a study published in 1988. The present report reviews data for 29 denominations from 1968 to 1997 that include 30 million full or confirmed members, and just over 100,000 of the estimated 350,000 religious congregations in the U.S.

The findings of the present church member giving analysis include the following.

- Giving as a percentage of income for a composite set of 29 denominations posted overall declines to Total Contributions and the two subcategories of Congregational Finances and Benevolences between 1968 and 1997. Giving as a percentage of income to Total Contributions and Congregational Finances declined from 1996 to 1997. Although giving as a percentage of income to Benevolences measured the same level in 1996 and 1997, the unrounded numbers indicated an increase for the first time in twelve years.

- When the composite set of 29 denominations was expanded to include a total of 43 Protestant communions, and data was compared for 1996-1997, giving as a percentage of income increased for all three categories. The increase to Benevolences measured slightly higher among the 29 denominations than in the expanded group of 43 communions.

- An analysis of data for a subset of mainline Protestant denominations and a subset of evangelical Protestant denominations found giving higher in the evangelical Protestant denominations, but a steeper decline in giving patterns among the evangelicals over the 1968-1996 period. Although the evangelical denominations were increasing in membership during these years, their members were giving a smaller contribution as a portion of income. The mainline denominations increased contributions as a percent of income to Congregational Finances between 1985 and 1997, while a continuing decline to Benevolences was evident.

- A review of giving patterns in 11 Protestant denominations from 1921 to 1997 found per member giving as a portion of income was above 3% from 1922 through 1933, the depth of the Great Depression. Giving recovered after World War II. Giving again began to decline in the early 1960s. Giving as a percentage of income was lower in 1997 than in either 1921 or 1933.

- Data for 1968-1985 was analyzed using both linear and exponential regression. Then 1986-1997 data was compared to the resulting trends. Both linear and exponential regression closely describe per member giving as a portion of income to Benevolences. Congregational Finances more closely resembled the exponential curve. Membership as a portion of U.S. population in 10 mainline denominations was best described by an exponential curve, while membership as a portion of U.S. population for the 29

1

denominations resembled the linear regression trend more closely. Data for a broad set of 38 denominations indicated that membership in the historically Christian church in the U.S. is shrinking as a portion of population.

- The potential for church giving levels was calculated. The results suggested that church members have sizable resources available, in theory, to apply to domestic and global needs.

- Currently available estimates of charitable activity in the United States may, unintentionally, be overreporting the level of activity. The annual rate of change in the data set of 29 denominations was used to develop a total giving to religion series keyed to the 1974 Filer Commission estimate of giving to religion. This series was compared to the American Association of Fund Raising Counsel, Inc. (AAFRC) *Giving USA* series. The AAFRC series includes data for years when AAFRC added to religion any difference between their total giving estimate and the sum of its use category estimates. The AAFRC series was higher than the denomination-based series. Recommendations are made as to how to develop a more academically-sound estimate for giving figures.

- In the last chapter, the need for creative church policy is explored. Church leaders often present only buildings and endowments as reasons for significantly increasing giving. Both agendas suggest an institutional maintenance approach. A mathematical model demonstrates that investing immediately in human beings may have more benefits than investing in endowments, in the latter instance, helping people by releasing funds slowly over an extended period of time.

# INTRODUCTION _____

How does one accumulate data for approximately 100,000 of the estimated 350,000 religious organizations in the United States?

The individual congregations initially provided the data to the regional or national denominational office with which the congregation is affiliated. The denominational offices then compiled the data. The *Yearbook of American and Canadian Churches* (*YACC*), of the National Council of the Churches of Christ in the U.S.A., requested the data from the national denominational offices, publishing it in annual YACC editions.

The data published by the *YACC*, in some cases combined with data obtained directly from a denominational source (as noted in the series of tables in Appendix B), serves as the basis for the present report. The numbers on the following pages are not survey reports. Rather, they represent the records turned in by pastors and lay congregational leaders to their own denominational offices.

By following the same data set over a period of years, trends can be seen among a particular set of church members. In addition, since the data set includes communions from across the theological spectrum, subsets of denominations within the larger grouping provide a basis for comparing patterns between communions with different perspectives.

Efforts are continually being made to use the latest information available. As a result, *The State of Church Giving through 1997* provides the most complete information available to date.

***Definition of Terms.*** The analyses in this report use certain terms that are defined as follows.

Full or Confirmed Members are used in the present analysis because it is a relatively consistent category among the reporting denominations. Certain denominations also report a larger figure for Inclusive Membership, which may include, for example, children who have been baptized but are not yet eligible for confirmation in that denomination. In this report, when the term "per member" is used, it refers to Full or Confirmed Members, unless otherwise noted.

Total Contributions Per Member refers to the average contribution in either dollars or as a percentage of income which is donated to the denominations' affiliated congregations by Full or Confirmed Members in a given year.

Total Contributions combines two subcategories of Congregational Finances and Benevolences. The definitions used in this report for the two subcategories are consistent with the standardized *YACC* data request questionnaire.

The first subcategory is Congregational Finances, which includes contributions directed to the internal operation of the individual congregation, including such items as the utility bills and salaries for the pastor and office staff, as well as Sunday school materials and capital programs.

The other subcategory is Benevolences. This category includes contributions for the congregation's external expenditures, beyond its own operations, for what might be termed the larger mission of the church. Benevolences includes international missions as well as national and local charities, through denominational channels as well as programs of nondenominational organizations to which the congregation contributes directly. Benevolences also includes support of denominational administration at all levels, as well as donations to denominational seminaries and schools.

As those familiar with congregational dynamics know, an individual generally donates an amount to the congregation which goes for Congregational Finances and Benevolences. During the budget preparation process, congregational leadership considers allocations to these categories. The budget may or may not be reviewed by all the congregation's members, depending on the communion's polity. However, the sum of the congregation's activities serves as a basis for members' decisions about whether to increase or decrease giving from one year to the next. Also, many congregations provide opportunities to designate directly to either Congregational Finances or Benevolences, through fund-raising drives, capital campaigns, and special offerings. Therefore, the allocations between Congregational Finances and Benevolences can be seen to fairly represent the priorities of church members.

When the terms "income," "per capita income," and "giving as a percentage of income" are used, they refer to the U.S. Per Capita Disposable (after-tax) Personal Income series from the U.S. Department of Commerce Bureau of Economic Analysis (BEA), unless otherwise noted.

The Implicit Price Deflator for Gross National Product was used to convert current dollars to 1992 dollars, thus factoring out inflation, unless otherwise specified.

Appendix C includes both U.S. Per Capita Disposable Personal Income figures and the Implicit Price Deflator for Gross National Product figures used in this study.

***Analysis Factors. Chained Dollars. The analyses in The State of Church*** *Giving* *through 1997 are keyed to the U.S. BEA series of "chained (1992) dollars." T*his series provides " 'chain-type annual-weighted' measures."[1] In October 1995, the U.S. BEA changed the benchmark year from 1987 to 1992 "because that is the latest year for which the current-dollar estimates will not be subject to revision until the next comprehensive revision."[2]

*Income Series*. The U.S. Department of Commerce Bureau of Economic Analysis has been in the process of publishing a revised income series, in conjunction with its

---

[1] *Survey of Current Business*, October 1995, page 30.

[2] *Survey of Current Business*, October 1995, page 30, footnote 3.

comprehensive revision. The U.S. Per Capita Disposable Personal Income data used in the present The State of Church Giving through 1997 includes a revised 1929-1981 series that was published by the U.S. BEA in 1998. The revised 1982 through 1996 series was published by the U.S. BEA in August of 1998. Because of these income revisions, the information in The State of Church Giving through 1997 is not strictly comparable with previous editions in the series before The State of Church Giving through 1996.

*Rate of Change Calculations, 1985-1997.* The following methodology is used to calculate the rate of change between 1985 and the most recent calendar year for which data is available, in the present case, 1997.

The rate of change between 1968 and 1985 was calculated by subtracting the 1968 giving as a percentage of income figure from the 1985 figure and then dividing the result by the 1968 figure.

The rate of change between 1985 and 1997 was calculated as follows. The 1968 giving as a percentage of income figure was subtracted from the 1997 figure and divided by the 1968 figure, producing a 1968-1997 rate of change. Then, the 1968-1985 rate of change was subtracted from the 1968-1997 figure. The result is the 1985-1997 rate of change, which may then be compared to the 1968-1985 figure.

*Rounding Calculations.* In most cases, Total Contributions, Total Congregational Finances, and Total Benevolences for the denominations being considered were divided by Full or Confirmed Membership in order to obtain per capita, or per member, data for that set of denominations. This procedure occasionally led to a small rounding discrepancy in one of the three related figures. That is, by a small margin, rounded per capita Total Contributions did not equal per capita Congregational Finances plus per capita Benevolences. Similarly, rounding data to the nearest dollar for use in tables and graphics led on occasion to a small rounding error in the data presented in tabular or graphic form.

*Giving in Dollars.* Per member giving to churches can be measured in dollars. The dollar measure indicates, among other information, how much money religious institutions have to spend. Did congregations have as much to spend in 1997 as they did in 1968? This question can be considered in both current dollars and inflation-adjusted dollars.

Current dollars indicate the value of the dollar in the year it was donated. However, since inflation changes the amount of goods or services that can be purchased with that dollar, data provided in current dollars has limited information value over a time span. If someone donated $5 in 1968 and $5 in 1997, on one level that person is donating the same amount of money. On another level, however, the buying power of that $5 has changed a great deal. Since less can be bought with the $5 donated in 1997 because of inflation in the economy, on a practical level the value of the donation has shrunk.

To account for the changes caused by inflation in the value of the dollar, a deflator can be applied. The result is inflation-adjusted 1992 dollars. Dollars adjusted to their chain-type, annual-weighted measure through the use of a deflator can be compared in terms of real growth over a time span since inflation has been factored out.

The deflator most commonly applied in this analysis designated the base period as 1992, with levels in 1992 set equal to 100. Thus, when adjusted by the deflator, the 1968 gift of $5 was worth $18.08 in inflation-adjusted 1992 dollars, and the 1997 gift of $5 was worth $4.48 in inflation-adjusted 1992 dollars.

***Giving as a Percentage of Income.*** There is another way to look at church member giving. This category is giving as a percentage of income. Considering what percentage or portion of income is donated to the religious congregation provides a different perspective. Rather than indicating how much money the congregation has to spend, as when one considers dollars donated, giving as a percentage of income indicates how the congregation rates in light of church members' total available incomes. Has the church sustained the same level of support from its members in comparison to previous years, as measured by what portion of income is being donated by members from the total resources available to them?

Percentage of income is a valuable measure because incomes change. Just as inflation changes the value of the dollar so $5 in 1968 is not the same as $5 in 1997, incomes, influenced by inflation and real growth, also change. For example, per capita income in 1968 was $3,101 in current dollars; if a church member gave $310 that year, that member would have been tithing, or giving the standard of ten percent. In contrast, 1997 per capita income had increased to $21,633 in current dollars; and if that church member still gave $310, the member would have been giving only about 1% of income. The church would have commanded a smaller portion of the member's overall income.

Thus, while dollars donated indicate how much the church has to spend, giving as a percentage of income provides some measure of the church member's level of commitment to the church in comparison to other spending priorities. One might say that giving as a percentage of income is an indication of the church's "market share" of church members' lives.

In most cases, to obtain giving as a percentage of income, total income to a set of denominations was divided by the number of Full or Confirmed Members in the set. This yielded the per member giving amount in dollars. This per member giving amount was divided by per capita disposable personal income.

***Data Appendix and Revisions.*** Appendix B includes the denominational data used in the analyses in this study. In general, the data for the denominations included in these analyses appears as it was reported in editions of the *YACC*. In some cases, data for one or more years for a specific denomination was obtained directly from the denominational office or another denominational source. Also, the denominational giving data set has been refined and revised as additional information has become available. Where relevant, this information is noted in the appendix.

Christian giving is God's divine plan to make us like Himself;
it reveals our religion and bares our souls . . .
— Warren H. Denison

chapter 1
## HIGHLIGHTS

# Church Member Giving, 1968-1997

Church giving is one indicator of the value that members place on their religion. Because denominational officials have obtained and aggregated giving within their communions, and then forwarded it to the *Yearbook of American and Canadian Churches* (*YACC*) office each year, data is available to consider the place of religion in members' lives over a period of decades.

***Introductory Comments.*** When a dollar is given to the church, it is allocated into one of two major subcategories, according to the annual form of the *YACC*. Congregational Finances refers to those expenditures that support the operation of the local congregation. Benevolences refers to expenditures for what might be termed the broader mission of the church, supporting everything from denominational offices to the local soup kitchen, from seminaries to international ministries.

Data is available for a set of denominations that have faithfully reported membership and giving information for a span of 30 years.

Giving can be considered from two points of view. The number of dollars given by members indicates how much money the church has to spend. Giving as a percentage of income, on the other hand, places donations in the larger context of income available to church members.

First, consider giving in terms of dollars given on a per member basis. Within the category of dollars given, there are two approaches as well: (1) current dollars; and (2) inflation-adjusted dollars.

Because inflation affects the value of dollars, a dollar in 1997 bought fewer goods or services than it did in 1968, an issue that seems difficult for members to understand at church although it becomes clear at the grocery store. In order to account for this factor, giving in dollars can be considered as current dollars (the value the dollars had in the year they were donated), or as inflation-adjusted dollars, factoring out the economic impact of inflation.

***Current Dollars, 1968-1997.*** Overall, from 1968 to 1997, Total Contributions to the church in current dollars increased $457.61 on a per member basis. Of this amount, $389.84 was directed to increase the per member Congregational Finances expenditures. Benevolences, or outreach, activities of the congregation, increased by $67.77.

Congregational Finances increased faster than Benevolences. Therefore, in 1968, 21¢ of each dollar went to Benevolences. By 1997, the amount had decreased to 16¢.

***Inflation-adjusted Dollars, 1968-1997.*** In inflation-adjusted 1992 dollars, per member giving to Total Contributions increased 42%, Congregational Finances increased 51%, and Benevolences increased 7%. Of the total inflation-adjusted dollar increase between 1968 and 1997, 96% was directed to Congregational Finances. This emphasis on the internal operations of the congregation helps explain the finding that Benevolences represented 21¢ of each dollar supporting church activity in 1968, and 16¢ in 1997.

**Figure 1:** Per Member Giving in Current and Inflation-Adjusted 1992 Dollars, 1968-1997_____

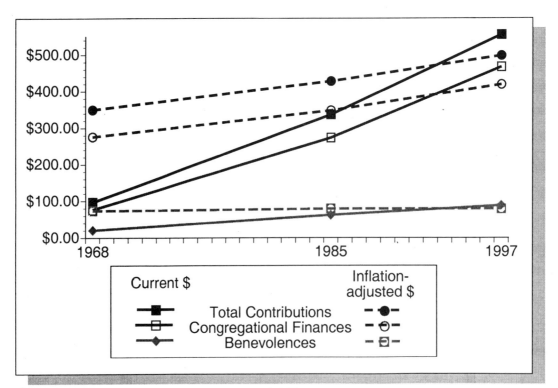

Source: empty tomb analysis; *YACC* adjusted series; U.S. BEA                    empty tomb, inc. 1999

*Giving as a Percentage of Income, 1968-1997.* The second approach to considering giving is as a portion of income. Unlike dollars, there is no distinction between current or inflation-adjusted dollars when one is considering giving as a percentage of income. So long as one compares current dollar giving to current dollar income when calculating the percentage of income—or inflation-adjusted giving with inflation-adjusted income—the percentage will be the same.

Between 1968 and 1997, per member giving as a percentage of income to Total Contributions decreased 18%. Even though per member Total Contributions increased 42% in inflation-adjusted dollars from 1968 to 1997, U.S. per capita disposable personal income increased 73% during the same period. The difference in the rate of increase between dollars contributed and per capita income explains how church member contributions could be increasing in inflation-adjusted dollars in most of the years from 1968 to 1997, and yet decreasing as a percentage of income in most of the years from 1968 to 1997.

Giving as a percentage of income to Total Contributions decreased from year to year 76% of the time between 1968 and 1997.

Congregational Finances decreased from year to year 66% of the time between 1968 and 1997. By 1997, Congregational Finances declined 12% from the 1968 base as a portion of income.

**Figure 2:** Per Member Giving as a Percent of Income, 1968-1997 _____

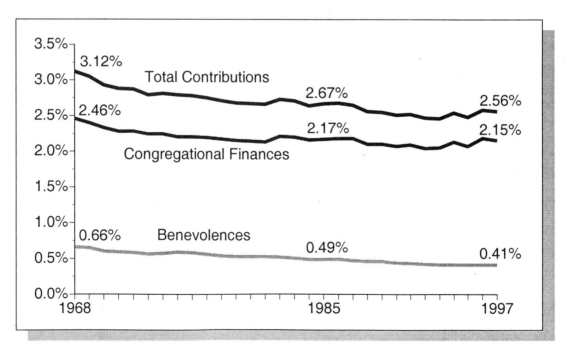

Source: empty tomb analysis; *YACC* adjusted series; U.S. BEA          empty tomb, inc. 1999

Benevolences declined 38% as a portion of income from 1968 to 1997. Benevolences declined from year to year 83% of the time.

In terms of giving from 1996 to 1997, both Total Contributions and Congregational Finances declined as a portion of income. In contrast, Benevolences broke an 11-year pattern of decline. Although the level of giving rounded to 0.41% in both years, the unrounded numbers suggested a slight increase from 1996 to 1997.

Apart from the overall decline in giving as a percentage of income, how much would have been donated if church members had given at least the same portion of income to their churches in 1997 as they did in 1968? In that case, members would have given $674.76 rather than $554.30. On an aggregate level, that would have meant the communions in the data set would have totaled $20.1 billion in Total Contributions rather than $16.5 billion. Congregational Finances would have received $15.9 billion, rather than $13.9 billion. Benevolences would have received $4.2 billion, rather than $2.6 billion, or 61% more money to further the larger purposes of the church.

## NARRATIVE

Tracking giving patterns in a set of denominations provides one basis to review how the church is faring, compared to other areas in which church members also invest their lives.

*Twenty-nine Denominations.* The first study that provided a basis for the present series was published in 1988. The *Yearbook of American and Canadian Churches* (*YACC*) series publishes church member giving data. Data for the years 1968 and 1985 could be confirmed for 31 denominations.[1] The data year 1968 was selected because, beginning that year, a consistent distinction was made between Full or Confirmed Membership and Inclusive Membership in the *YACC* series. The denominations that published data for both 1968 and 1985 included 29,442,390 Full or Confirmed Members in 1985. They comprise approximately 100,000 of the estimated 350,000 religious congregations in the U.S.

The present church member giving report series extended the analysis for the original set of denominations beyond 1985. The current report analyzes the data set, now comprising 29 denominations, through 1997, the most recent year for which data was available at the time the report was written.[2] Also, data for the intervening years of 1969 through 1984, and 1986 through 1996, was included

[1] John Ronsvalle and Sylvia Ronsvalle, *A Comparison of the Growth in Church Contributions with United States Per Capita Income* (Champaign, IL: empty tomb, inc., 1988).

[2] Two of the original 31 denominations merged in 1987, bringing the total number of denominations in the original data set to 30. As of 1991, one denomination reported that it no longer had the staff to collect national financial data, resulting in a maximum of 29 denominations from the original set which could provide data for 1991 through 1996.

One of these 29 denominations did not have comprehensive financial information for the years 1996 through 1997 at the time the present report was drafted, but plans to in time for the next edition of this study. Therefore, throughout this report, what was an original set of 31 denominations in 1985 is referred to as a set of 29 denominations, reflecting the denominations' 1995 composition, although data for 31 denominations is included for 1968 and 1985, as well as for intervening years, as available.

in the composite data set, as available.[3]

In reviewing church member giving, at least two approaches can be taken. First, the number of dollars given by members indicates how much money the church has to spend. However, the number of dollars given do not take into account the level of changing resources available to the church member.

Giving as a percentage of income, on the other hand, places donations in the larger context of income available to church members. Incomes change by both inflation and also real growth. Church members in the mid-1990s were deciding how much to give from a different income base than did people in the late 1960s. In 1997, were church members directing the same portion of their incomes to their churches as did members three decades ago? The percentage of income gives a measure of the church's "market share" of members' lifestyles.

***Church Giving in Current Dollars.*** Calculating contributions on a per member basis accounts for any changes in membership, either through growth or decline, that might have taken place during the period under review. The number of dollars donated by members indicates how much the church had to spend on both local institutional operations, as well as what might be termed its larger mission.

One major factor must be considered when reviewing giving in terms of dollar amounts. Because inflation affects the value of dollars, a dollar in 1997 bought fewer goods or services than it did in 1968.

In order to account for this factor, giving in dollars can be considered from two points of view: current dollars (the value the dollars had in the year they were donated); and inflation-adjusted dollars, factoring out the economic impact of inflation.

Table 1 presents the data for the per member contribution in dollars for the composite group of denominations included in the data set in both current and inflation-adjusted dollars.

Each data series is considered in three categories. Total Contributions Per Member represents the average total contribution for each full or confirmed church member in the composite 29 denominations. This

Total Contributions figure combines two subcategories: Congregational Finances (which includes the monies the congregation spent on internal operations); and Benevolences (which includes what might be termed the larger mission of the church, such as local, national and international missions, as well as denominational support and seminary funding, among other items).

It may be noted that the per member amount given to Total Contributions increased in current dollars each year during the 1968-1997 period. The portion of Total Contributions Per Member which stayed in the congregation to fund Congregational Finances also went up each year. In this same period, current dollar per member contributions to Benevolences declined only once, from 1969 to 1970. Otherwise, giving to Benevolences also increased each year.

Overall, from 1968 to 1997, Total Contributions to the church in current dollars increased $457.61 on a per member basis. Of this amount, $389.84 was directed to increase the per member Congregational Finances expenditures, for the benefit of members within the congregation. Benevolences, or outreach, activities of the congregation, increased by $67.77. On a current dollar basis, 15% of the total increase from 1968 to 1997 was directed to Benevolences.

One effect of this allocation was that Benevolences shrank as a portion of Total Contributions. In 1968, 21¢ of each dollar went to Benevolences. By 1997, the amount had decreased to 16¢. Further, when inflation was factored out, it was clear that churches were carrying out Benevolences in 1997 with only a slightly higher level of resources per member than those available to fund these activities in 1968.

***Church Giving in Inflation-Adjusted Dollars.*** The United States Bureau of Economic Analysis (U.S. BEA) periodically revises the deflator series that are used to factor out inflation. These deflators allow dollar figures to be compared more precisely across years. The current year of base comparison in the U.S. BEA series is 1992.[4] By applying the Implicit Price Deflator for Gross National Product to the current dollar church member giving data, the data can be reviewed across years with inflation factored out. The

---

[3] For 1986 through 1997, annual denominational data has been obtained which represented for any given year at least 99.31% of the 1985 Full or Confirmed Membership of the denominations included in the 1968-1985 study. For 1986 through 1997, the number of denominations for which data was available varied from a low of 25 in 1986 to a high of 29 in 1991 through 1995. For the years 1969 through 1984, the number of denominations varied from a low of 23 in 1970 to 29 in 1983, representing at least 98.98% of the

membership in the data set. The denominational giving data considered in this analysis was obtained either from the *Yearbook of American and Canadian Churches* series, or directly in correspondence with a denominational office. For a full listing of the data used in this analysis, including the sources, see Appendix B-1.

[4] See the section titled "Revised Analysis Factors" in the Introduction for further detail.

**Table 1:** Per Member Giving to Total Contributions, Congregational Finances and Benevolences, Current and Inflation-Adjusted 1992 Dollars, 1968-1997

| | Per Full or Confirmed Member Giving to Congregations, in Dollars | | | | | | | | |
|---|---|---|---|---|---|---|---|---|---|
| | *Current Dollars* | | | Inflation-Adjusted 1992 Dollars | | | | | |
| Year | Total | Cong. Finances | Benevol. | Total | ↑↓ | Cong. Finances | ↑↓ | Benevol. | ↑↓ |
| 1968 | *$96.69* | *$76.33* | *$20.37* | $349.58 | | $275.94 | | $73.64 | |
| 1969 | *$100.74* | *$79.14* | *$21.59* | $347.84 | ↓ | $273.28 | ↓ | $74.56 | ↑ |
| 1970 | *$104.19* | *$82.76* | *$21.43* | $341.60 | ↓ | $271.35 | ↓ | $70.25 | ↓ |
| 1971 | *$109.58* | *$87.06* | *$22.52* | $341.58 | ↓ | $271.38 | ↑ | $70.20 | ↓ |
| 1972 | *$117.10* | *$93.26* | *$23.84* | $350.17 | ↑ | $278.87 | ↑ | $71.29 | ↑ |
| 1973 | *$127.44* | *$102.07* | *$25.37* | $360.82 | ↑ | $289.00 | ↑ | $71.82 | ↑ |
| 1974 | *$138.92* | *$110.82* | *$28.10* | $360.92 | ↑ | $287.93 | ↓ | $73.00 | ↑ |
| 1975 | *$150.13* | *$118.37* | *$31.76* | $356.52 | ↓ | $281.10 | ↓ | $75.42 | ↑ |
| 1976 | *$162.84* | *$129.09* | *$33.75* | $365.28 | ↑ | $289.57 | ↑ | $75.71 | ↑ |
| 1977 | *$175.70* | *$140.08* | *$35.62* | $370.21 | ↑ | $295.15 | ↑ | $75.06 | ↓ |
| 1978 | *$192.87* | *$154.57* | *$38.30* | $378.78 | ↑ | $303.55 | ↑ | $75.22 | ↑ |
| 1979 | *$211.46* | *$169.50* | *$41.96* | $382.67 | ↑ | $306.73 | ↑ | $75.93 | ↑ |
| 1980 | *$232.42* | *$186.07* | *$46.35* | $385.06 | ↑ | $308.26 | ↑ | $76.79 | ↑ |
| 1981 | *$255.50* | *$204.38* | *$51.12* | $386.82 | ↑ | $309.43 | ↑ | $77.39 | ↑ |
| 1982 | *$276.15* | *$223.63* | *$52.52* | $393.33 | ↑ | $318.52 | ↑ | $74.81 | ↓ |
| 1983 | *$292.32* | *$236.88* | *$55.44* | $399.34 | ↑ | $323.61 | ↑ | $75.74 | ↑ |
| 1984 | *$314.99* | *$256.74* | *$58.25* | $414.62 | ↑ | $337.95 | ↑ | $76.68 | ↑ |
| 1985 | *$336.00* | *$272.93* | *$62.32* | $427.64 | ↑ | $347.37 | ↑ | $79.32 | ↑ |
| 1986 | *$353.72* | *$288.50* | *$65.22* | $438.75 | ↑ | $357.85 | ↑ | $80.90 | ↑ |
| 1987 | *$367.08* | *$301.32* | *$65.76* | $441.79 | ↑ | $362.65 | ↑ | $79.14 | ↓ |
| 1988 | *$381.53* | *$312.56* | *$68.98* | $443.03 | ↑ | $362.93 | ↑ | $80.09 | ↑ |
| 1989 | *$402.67* | *$330.79* | *$71.88* | $448.65 | ↑ | $368.57 | ↑ | $80.08 | ↓ |
| 1990 | *$419.06* | *$346.16* | *$72.90* | $447.57 | ↓ | $369.71 | ↑ | $77.85 | ↓ |
| 1991 | *$433.28* | *$358.60* | *$74.69* | $445.17 | ↓ | $368.43 | ↓ | $76.74 | ↓ |
| 1992 | *$444.74* | *$368.19* | *$76.56* | $444.74 | ↓ | $368.19 | ↓ | $76.56 | ↓ |
| 1993 | *$457.22* | *$380.47* | *$76.75* | $445.50 | ↑ | $370.72 | ↑ | $74.78 | ↓ |
| 1994 | *$488.54* | *$409.26* | *$79.28* | $464.92 | ↑ | $389.48 | ↑ | $75.44 | ↑ |
| 1995 | *$497.51* | *$415.97* | *$81.54* | $462.84 | ↓ | $386.98 | ↓ | $75.86 | ↑ |
| 1996 | *$537.99* | *$453.37* | *$84.62* | $491.32 | ↑ | $414.04 | ↑ | $77.28 | ↑ |
| 1997 | *$554.30* | *$466.16* | *$88.14* | $497.04 | ↑ | $418.01 | ↑ | $79.04 | ↑ |

Details in the above table may not compute to the numbers shown due to rounding.

result of this process is also listed in Table 1. The arrows next to the three inflation-adjusted columns are intended to provide a visual indicator as to whether giving increased or decreased from one year to the next.

When the effects of inflation are removed in the 1968 to 1997 giving amounts, one may note that per member giving decreased in more years than in the current dollar columns. For example, although per member contributions to Total Contributions increased in the majority of years, the years 1969 through 1971, 1975, 1990 through 1992, and 1995 posted declines.

Congregational Finances also generally increased in inflation-adjusted 1992 dollars. Declines only appear in seven years: 1969, 1970, 1974, 1975, 1991, 1992, and 1995.

Benevolences also increased in the majority of years. Decreases occurred in ten years in the 1968-1997 period, in the years 1970, 1971, 1977, 1982, 1987, and the five years, 1989 through 1993.

Figure 3 presents the changes in inflation-adjusted dollar contributions to the three categories of Total Contributions, Congregational Finances and Benevolences.

Over the 1968-1997 period, per member donations to Total Contributions in inflation-adjusted dollars increased from $349.58 to $497.04, an increase of $147.47, or 42%.

Of the total increase, $142.07 was directed to Congregational Finances. This subcategory increased 51% between 1968 and 1997, from $275.94 to $418.01.

In contrast, Benevolences increased $5.40, from $73.64 in 1968 to $79.04 in 1997. Thus, Benevolences increased an average of 7% per member between 1968 and 1997.

Of the total inflation-adjusted dollar increase between 1968 and 1997, 96% was directed to Congregational Finances. This emphasis on the internal operations of the congregation helps explain the finding that Benevolences represented 21% of all church activity in 1968, and 16% in 1997.

Figure 4 provides a comparison of per member giving to the categories of Congregational Finances and Benevolences with changes in U.S. per capita disposable personal income in inflation-adjusted 1992 dollars.

***Giving as a Percent of Income.*** U.S. per capita disposable (after-tax) personal income serves as an average income figure for the broad spectrum of church members included in the composite of 29 denominations.

U.S. per capita disposable personal income was $3,101 in current dollars in 1968. When that figure is calculated in inflation-adjusted 1992 dollars, U.S. per capita disposable personal income in 1968 was $11,211.

The current-dollar income figure for 1997 was $21,633. When inflation was factored out, 1997 U.S. per capita disposable personal income was $19,398.

Thus, per capita income in inflation-adjusted dollars increased by $8,187, an increase of 73% from 1968 to 1997.

**Figure 3:** Changes in Per Member Giving in Inflation-Adjusted 1992 Dollars, Total Contributions, Congregational Finances, and Benevolences, 1968-1997

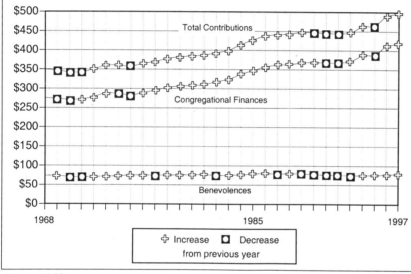

Sources: *YACC*, adjusted series; U.S. BEA

empty tomb, inc. 1999

**Figure 4:** Per Member Giving to Congregational Finances and Benevolences, and U.S. Per Capita Personal Income, 1968-1997, Inflation-Adjusted 1992 Dollars

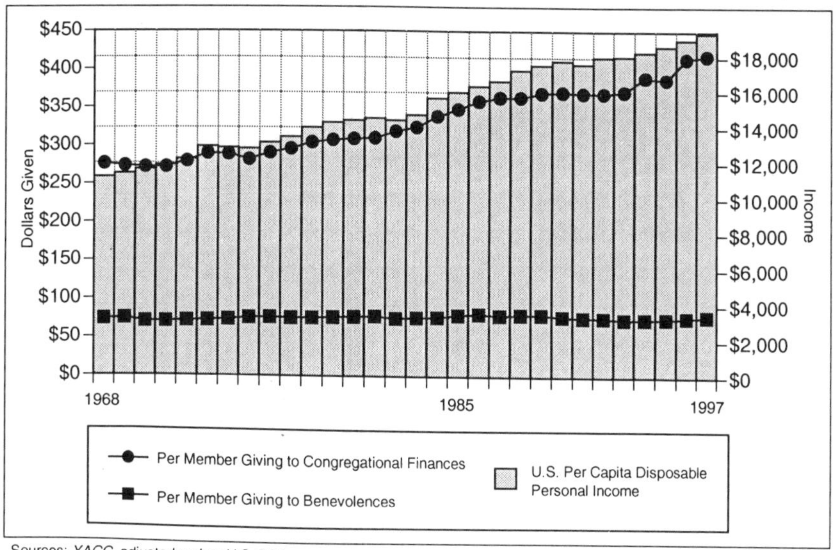

Sources: *YACC*, adjusted series; U.S. BEA

empty tomb, inc. 1999

In Table 2, giving as a percentage of income is presented for per member Total Contributions, and the related subcategories of Congregational Finances and Benevolences. As in Table 1 the arrows indicate whether the percentage of income in that category increased or decreased from the previous year. Inasmuch as the percent figures are rounded to the second decimal place, the arrows indicate the direction of a slight increase or decrease for those situations in which the percentage provided appears to be the same numerical figure as the previous year.

While Table 1 presents data in both current and inflation-adjusted dollars, Table 2 lists a single set of data for giving as a percentage of income. There is no distinction between current or inflation-adjusted dollars when one is considering giving as a percentage of income. The same procedures are applied to both the giving and income dollar amounts when converting

**Table 2:** Per Member Giving as a Percentage of Income, 1968-1997

| Per Full or Confirmed Member Giving to Congregations as a Percentage of Income | | | | | | |
|---|---|---|---|---|---|---|
| Year | Total Contributions Per Member | ↑↓ | Congregational Finances | ↑↓ | Benevolences | ↑↓ |
| 1968 | 3.12% |  | 2.46% |  | 0.66% |  |
| 1969 | 3.05% | ↓ | 2.40% | ↓ | 0.65% | ↓ |
| 1970 | 2.93% | ↓ | 2.33% | ↓ | 0.60% | ↓ |
| 1971 | 2.88% | ↓ | 2.28% | ↓ | 0.59% | ↓ |
| 1972 | 2.87% | ↓ | 2.28% | ↑ | 0.58% | ↓ |
| 1973 | 2.79% | ↓ | 2.24% | ↓ | 0.56% | ↓ |
| 1974 | 2.81% | ↑ | 2.24% | ↑ | 0.57% | ↑ |
| 1975 | 2.79% | ↓ | 2.20% | ↓ | 0.59% | ↑ |
| 1976 | 2.78% | ↓ | 2.20% | ↑ | 0.58% | ↓ |
| 1977 | 2.75% | ↓ | 2.19% | ↓ | 0.56% | ↓ |
| 1978 | 2.71% | ↓ | 2.17% | ↓ | 0.54% | ↓ |
| 1979 | 2.68% | ↓ | 2.15% | ↓ | 0.53% | ↓ |
| 1980 | 2.67% | ↓ | 2.14% | ↓ | 0.53% | ↑ |
| 1981 | 2.66% | ↓ | 2.13% | ↓ | 0.53% | ↓ |
| 1982 | 2.73% | ↑ | 2.21% | ↑ | 0.52% | ↓ |
| 1983 | 2.71% | ↓ | 2.20% | ↓ | 0.51% | ↓ |
| 1984 | 2.64% | ↓ | 2.16% | ↓ | 0.49% | ↓ |
| 1985 | 2.67% | ↑ | 2.17% | ↑ | 0.49% | ↑ |
| 1986 | 2.68% | ↑ | 2.18% | ↑ | 0.49% | ↓ |
| 1987 | 2.65% | ↓ | 2.18% | ↓ | 0.47% | ↓ |
| 1988 | 2.56% | ↓ | 2.10% | ↓ | 0.46% | ↓ |
| 1989 | 2.55% | ↓ | 2.10% | ↓ | 0.46% | ↓ |
| 1990 | 2.51% | ↓ | 2.07% | ↓ | 0.44% | ↓ |
| 1991 | 2.52% | ↑ | 2.09% | ↑ | 0.43% | ↓ |
| 1992 | 2.47% | ↓ | 2.04% | ↓ | 0.42% | ↓ |
| 1993 | 2.46% | ↓ | 2.05% | ↑ | 0.41% | ↓ |
| 1994 | 2.54% | ↑ | 2.13% | ↑ | 0.41% | ↓ |
| 1995 | 2.48% | ↓ | 2.07% | ↓ | 0.41% | ↓ |
| 1996 | 2.58% | ↑ | 2.18% | ↑ | 0.41% | ↓ |
| 1997 | 2.56% | ↓ | 2.15% | ↓ | 0.41% | ↑ |

Details in the above table may not compute to the numbers shown due to rounding.

current dollars into inflation-adjusted dollars. As long as one compares current dollar giving to current dollar per capita income when calculating the percentage of income, and inflation-adjusted dollar giving to inflation-adjusted dollar per capita income while using the same deflator, the percentages of income will be the same.

A review of Table 2 yields the following information.

Overall, per member giving as a percentage of income to Total Contributions decreased from 3.12% to 2.56%, a decline of 18%. Giving as a percentage of income to Total Contributions decreased 21 times out of a possible 29 times, or 76% of the time.

The trends differ from giving in dollars. The review of the dollar numbers in Table 1 indicated that per member giving increased in both current and inflation-adjusted dollars. However, when that dollar giving is considered in light of changes to income, a different picture emerges. While church members increased the amount of dollars they donated to the church between 1968 through 1997, the rate of increase in the number of dollars donated was not comparable to the rate of increase in U.S. per capita income. Per member Total Contributions increased 42% in inflation-adjusted dollars from 1968 to 1997. However, U.S. per capita disposable personal income increased 73% during the same period.

The difference in the rate of increase between dollars contributed and per capita income explains how church member contributions could be increasing in inflation-adjusted dollars in most of the years from 1968 to 1997, and yet decreasing as a percentage of income in most of the years from 1968 to 1997.

Evaluating the dollars donated in the context of changes in income results in the finding that the portion of income members directed to their churches decreased by 18% during the 1968 to 1997 period.

Congregational Finances as a portion

of income decreased 19 times during the 29 two-year sets in the 1968-1997 period, or 66% of the time. Congregational Finances declined from 2.46% in 1968 to 2.15% in 1997, a percent change of -12% from the 1968 base in giving as a percentage of income.

Benevolences declined from 0.66% of income in 1968 to 0.41% in 1997, a decline of 38% as a portion of income. Out of the 29 two-year sets in the 1968-1997 interval, the portion of income that went to Benevolences declined 24 times, or 83% of the time. However, a slight upturn was evident in giving to Benevolences from 1996 to 1997. Although per member giving measured 0.41% in both 1996 and 1997, a slight increase was evident in the unrounded numbers. This growth in Benevolences giving broke an 11-year pattern of decline in that category.

Figure 5 presents per member giving as a percentage of income to Congregational Finances and Benevolences, compared to U.S. per capita income.

***Giving in Inflation-adjusted Dollars, 1968, 1985 and 1997.*** The first report, that served as the basis for the present series on church member giving, considered data for the denominations in the composite for the years 1968 and 1985. With the data now available through 1997, a broader trend can be reviewed for the period under discussion, the 30-year range from 1968 to 1997.

The per member amount donated to Total Contributions in inflation-adjusted 1992 dollars was $78.06 greater in 1985 than it was in 1968 for the

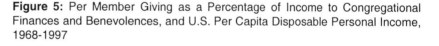

**Figure 5:** Per Member Giving as a Percentage of Income to Congregational Finances and Benevolences, and U.S. Per Capita Disposable Personal Income, 1968-1997

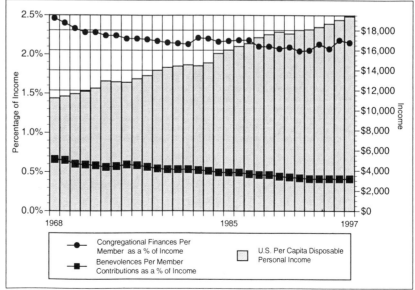

Sources: *YACC*, adjusted series; U.S. BEA

empty tomb, inc. 1999

denominations included in the data set, an average increase of $4.59 a year in per member contributions. There was an overall increase during the 1985-1997 twelve-year interval as well. In 1997, the per member contribution to the 29 denominations, which represented 99.31% of the total 1985 membership of the denominations originally studied, was $69.41 more per member in inflation-adjusted dollars than in 1985. The average annual increase was $5.78 between 1985 and 1997, a higher rate compared to the 1968-1985 average annual increase of $4.59.

Gifts to Congregational Finances also increased between 1968 and 1985, as well as from 1985 to 1997. As in the case of Total Contributions, the annual rate of increase accelerated. Per member contributions to Congregational Finances were $275.94 in 1968, in inflation-adjusted 1992 dollars, and had increased to $347.37 in 1985, a total increase of $71.43, with an average rate of change of $4.20. From 1985 to 1997, the average annual rate of change increased to $5.89, with per member gifts growing from $347.37 in 1985 to $418.01 in 1997, an increase of $70.64. Congregational Finances increased more than Total Contributions between 1985 and 1997, accompanied by a decline in giving to Benevolences.

In inflation-adjusted 1992 dollars, gifts to Benevolences were $73.64 in 1968 and grew to $79.32 in 1985, an increase of $5.68, with an annual average rate of change of $0.33. Between 1985 and 1997, per member gifts to Benevolences declined to $79.04, a decrease of $0.28, with an annual average rate of change of -$0.02 for the 1985-1997 period, reversing the low growth trend evident between 1968 and 1985.

Table 3 presents per member gifts to Total Contributions, Congregational Finances and Benevolences in inflation-adjusted 1992 dollars for the years 1968, 1985 and 1997.

*Giving as a Percentage of Income, 1968, 1985 and 1997.* Between 1968 and 1985, Total Contributions declined from 3.12% to 2.67% as a portion of income. The percentage change in giving as a percentage of income from the 1968 base was -14.43% in the 17 years from 1968 to 1985.

From 1985 to 1997, giving as a percentage of income to Total Contributions changed from 2.67% in 1985 to 2.56% in 1997. The percentage change in giving as a percentage of income was -3.40% in this twelve-year interval. Therefore, the annual percent change in the portion of per capita income donated to Total Contributions was -0.28% in the 1985-1997 period, compared to the rate of -0.85% in the 1968-1985 period. This data suggests that the rate of annual decline in giving as a percentage of income decreased in the last twelve years of the 1968 to 1997 period.

Table 4 presents data for Total Contributions per member as a percentage of income in summary fashion for the years 1968, 1985 and 1997.

Per member gifts to Congregational Finances measured 2.46% of income in 1968, 2.17% in 1985 and 2.15% in 1997. The annual average percent change in giving as a percentage of income changed from -0.70% a year between 1968 and 1985, from the 1968 base, to -0.04% a year between 1985 and 1997. As with giving to Total Contributions, the data indicates a slowing in the annual rate of decline in giving as a percentage of income to Congregational Finances in the last twelve years of the 1968-1997 period.

Between 1985 and 1997, the annual average percent decline in giving as a percentage of income to Benevolences was smaller than that during the 1968-1985 period as well. From 1968 to 1985, the portion of member income directed to Benevolences decreased from 0.66% to 0.49%, an absolute decline of -0.16%. This figure translated to a percent change in giving as

**Table 3:** Total Contributions, Congregational Finances and Benevolences, Per Member Giving in Inflation-Adjusted 1992 Dollars, 1968, 1985 and 1997

| | Giving Per Member in Inflation-Adjusted 1992 Dollars | | | | | | | | |
| | Total Contributions | | | Congregational Finances | | | Benevolences | | |
| Year | Per Member Giving | Diff. from Previous $ Base | Average Annual Diff. in $s Given | Per Member Giving | Diff. from Previous $ Base | Average Annual Diff. in $s Given | Per Member Giving | Diff. from Previous $ Base | Average Annual Diff. in $s Given |
|---|---|---|---|---|---|---|---|---|---|
| 1968 | $349.58 | | | $275.94 | | | $73.64 | | |
| 1985 | $427.64 | $78.06 | $4.59 | $347.37 | $71.43 | $4.20 | $79.32 | $5.68 | $0.33 |
| 1997 | $497.04 | $69.41 | $5.78 | $418.01 | $70.64 | $5.89 | $79.04 | -$0.28 | -$0.02 |

Details in the above table may not compute to the numbers shown due to rounding.

**Table 4:** Per Member Giving as a Percentage of Income to Total Contributions, 1968, 1985 and 1997[5]

| Year | Total Contributions Per Member as a Percentage of Income | | | |
|---|---|---|---|---|
| | Total Contributions Per Member as a Percentage of Income | Difference in Total Contributions Per Member as a Percent of Income from Previous Base | Percent Change in Total Contributions Per Member as a Percent of Income Calculated from 1968 Base | Annual Average Percent Change in Total Contributions Per Member as a Percent of Income |
| 1968 | 3.12% | | | |
| 1985 | 2.67% | -0.45% | -14.43% from 1968 | -0.85% |
| 1997 | 2.56% | - 0.11% | - 3.40% from 1985 | - 0.28% |

Details in the above table may not compute to the numbers shown due to rounding.

**Table 5:** Per Member Giving as a Percentage of Income to Congregational Finances, 1968, 1985 and 1997

| Year | Congregational Finances Per Member as a Percentage of Income | | | |
|---|---|---|---|---|
| | Congregational Finances Per Member as a Percent of Income | Difference in Congregational Finances Per Member as a Percent of Income from Previous Base | Percent Change in Congregational Finances Per Member as a Percent of Income Calculated from 1968 Base | Annual Average Percent Change in Congregational Finances Per Member as a Percent of Income |
| 1968 | 2.46% | | | |
| 1985 | 2.17% | -0.29% | -11.94% from 1968 | -0.70% |
| 1997 | 2.15% | -0.01% | -0.51% from 1985 | -0.04% |

Details in the above table may not compute to the numbers shown due to rounding.

a percentage of income of -24.65% from the 1968 base, with an annual average percent change of -1.45%. In the twelve-year interval from 1985 to 1997, giving as a percentage of income directed to Benevolences declined from 0.49% to 0.41% between 1985 and 1997, an absolute drop of 0.09% during those twelve years, compared to a decline of 0.16% in the 17-year interval of 1968-1985. The 1985-1997 percent change in giving as a percentage of income of -13.32% produced an annual average percent change of -1.11%, compared to the 1968-1985 seventeen-year rate of -1.45%. Table 6 presents the data for Benevolences as a percentage of income in 1968, 1985 and 1997.

***Giving in 1996 Compared to 1997.*** Per member giving as a percentage of income to Total Contributions

in 1996 measured 2.58%. In 1997, the figure was 2.56%.

Congregational Finances also declined from 1996 to 1997, from 2.18% in 1996 to 2.15% in 1997.

From 1996 to 1997, Benevolences interrupted a multiyear pattern of decline. Although the level of giving rounded to 0.41% of income in both years, the unrounded numbers suggested a slight increase from 1996 to 1997.

***Potential Giving.*** The last chapter in this edition explores the potential consequences, had per member giving as a portion of income increased between 1968 and 1997. However, here the question may be considered, what would have been the situation in

---

[5] An explanation as to how the 1968-1985 and 1985-1997 rates of change were calculated may be found in the Introduction.

**Table 6:** Per Member Giving as a Percentage of Income to Benevolences, 1968, 1985 and 1997

| Year | Benevolences Per Member as a Percentage of Income | | | |
|------|---------------------------------------------------|---|---|---|
| | Benevolences Per Member as a Percent of Income | Difference in Benevolences Per Member as a Percent of Income from Previous Base | Percent Change in Benevolences Per Member as a Percent of Income Calculated from 1968 Base | Annual Average Percent Change in Benevolences Per Member as a Percent of Income |
| 1968 | 0.66% | | | |
| 1985 | 0.49% | -0.16% | -24.65% from 1968 | -1.45% |
| 1997 | 0.41% | - 0.09% | - 13.32% from 1985 | - 1.11% |

Details in the above table may not compute to the numbers shown due to rounding.

1997 if giving had at least maintained the 1968 percentages of income donated? Rather than the actual 1997 levels of giving, what if giving as a percentage of income in 1997 measured 3.12% for Total Contributions, 2.46% for Congregational Finances, and 0.66% for Benevolences, which were the levels of giving for these three categories in 1968?

Had that been true, per member giving to Total Contributions in current 1997 dollars would have been $674.76 instead of $554.30; Congregational Finances would have been $532.97 instead of $466.16; and Benevolences would have been $141.79 instead of $88.14.

The implications of these differences become clearer when the aggregate totals are calculated by multiplying the theoretical per member giving levels by the number of members reported by these denominations in 1997. Aggregate Total Contributions would then have been $20.1 billion rather than $16.5 billion, a difference of $3.6 billion, or an increase of 22%.

Aggregate Congregational Finances would have been $15.9 billion rather than $13.9 billion, a difference of $2 billion, or an increase of 14%.

There would have been a 61% increase in the total amount received for Benevolences. Instead of receiving $2.6 billion in 1997, as these denominations did, they would have received $4.2 billion, a difference of $1.6 billion.

*Summary.* When per member giving was considered in current dollar values, giving increased each year from 1968 to 1997 to Total Contributions and the subcategory of Congregational Finances. Per member giving also increased to Benevolences in every year except one.

When per member giving was considered in inflation-adjusted 1992 dollars, the majority of the years demonstrated increases to Total Contributions and the two subcategories of Congregational Finances and Benevolences. However, 96% of the increase in Total Contributions was directed to Congregational Finances. Benevolences therefore represented 21¢ of each church dollar in 1968, and 16¢ of each church dollar in 1997.

Giving as a percentage of income posted an overall decline between 1968 and 1997 for Total Contributions and the two subcategories of Congregational Finances and Benevolences. From year to year, the portion of income directed to Total Contributions declined 76% of the time, to Congregational Finances 66% of the time, and to Benevolences 83% of the time.

The average annual rate of decline in giving as a percentage of income to Total Contributions, Congregational Finances and Benevolences slowed in the 1985 to 1997 period compared to the 1968 to 1985 period.

From 1996 to 1997, the level of giving as a percentage of income to Total Contributions and Congregational Finances declined. However, while figures to the second decimal for giving as a percentage of income to Benevolences remained constant from 1996 to 1997, the unrounded data suggested a slight increase. This increase breaks an 11-year pattern of decline.

Had giving levels remained constant rather than declined as a portion of income from 1968 to 1997, aggregate donations to congregations would have been $3.6 billion greater in 1997.

## chapter 2
## HIGHLIGHTS_____

*Church Member Giving
for 43 Denominations,
1996 to 1997*

In addition to the denominations in the composite data set, a number of other denominations also provided data for 1996 and 1997 to the *Yearbook of American and Canadian Churches* series. When data for these additional communions was also included, the number in the analysis expanded to 43 denominations with 40 million members.

As with the composite group, per member giving in inflation-adjusted dollars increased for the expanded group of 43 denominations.

A different pattern was evident between the two sets for per member giving as a percentage of income to Total Contributions and Congregational Finances, however. Giving as a percentage of income decreased from 1996 to 1997 in the composite set, to both Total Contributions and Congregational Finances. In the expanded set, Total Contributions increased from 2.64% to 2.65%. Although the portion of income donated to Congregational Finances measured 2.21% in both 1996 and 1997 in the expanded set, the unrounded numbers indicated a slight increase.

In both the composite set and the expanded set, per member giving as a portion of income to Benevolences increased from 1996 to 1997. The composite set posted a slightly larger increase than did the expanded set.

# NARRATIVE

The 1968-1997 analysis in chapter one considers data for a group of denominations that published their membership and financial information for 1968 and 1985 in the *Yearbook of American and Canadian Churches (YACC)* series. That initial set of communions, considered in the first report on which the present series on church giving is based, has served as a denominational composite set analyzed for subsequent data years.

Data covering both 1996 and 1997 for an additional fifteen denominations was either published in the relevant editions of the *YACC* series, or obtained directly from denominational offices. By adding the data for these 15 denominations to that of the composite group for these two years, giving patterns in an expanded set of communions can be considered.

In this enlarged comparison, the member sample increased from 29.6 million to 40,410,696 Full or Confirmed Members, and the number of denominations increased from 28 to 43.[6] The larger group of denominations included both The United Methodist Church and The Episcopal Church, which were not included in the original 1968-1985 analysis because of the unavailability of confirmed 1968 data.[7] A list of the denominations included in the present analysis is contained in Appendix A.

***Per Member Giving in Inflation-Adjusted 1992 Dollars.*** As noted in the first chapter of this report, per member giving to Total Contributions increased from 1996 to 1997 for the composite group of 29 denominations in inflation-adjusted 1992 dollars. Specifically, Total Contributions Per Member increased by $5.73 in inflation-adjusted 1992 dollars, from $491.32 in 1996 to $497.04 in 1997. When the group was expanded to 43 denominations, Total Per Member giving increased by $10.20, from $503.32 in 1996 to $513.52 in 1997. The rate of giving was higher in the expanded set than in the composite group.

The composite group of denominations increased per member giving in inflation-adjusted dollars to Congregational Finances by $3.97, from $414.04 in 1996 to $418.01 in 1997. The expanded group increased by $8.44, from $420.66 in 1996 to $429.10 in 1997.

In both groups, giving to Benevolences also increased from 1996 to 1997. In the composite communions, per member contributions to Benevolences increased from $77.28 to $79.04, an increase of $1.76. The expanded group of 43 denominations also increased by $1.76, from $82.67 to $84.42.

Table 7 presents per member giving data for 1996 and 1997 for the expanded group of 43 denominations, both in inflation-adjusted 1992 dollars, and also as a percentage of income. In addition, the change from 1996 to 1997 in per member contributions in inflation-adjusted 1992 dollars, in giving as a percentage of income, and in the percent change in giving as a percentage of income from the 1996 base are also presented in the table.

***Per Member Giving as a Percentage of Income.*** In the composite denominations set, from 1996 to 1997, giving as a percentage of income decreased to Total Contributions and Congregational Finances, while there was a slight increase in giving to Benevolences. In this group, the percent given to Total Contributions decreased from 2.58% in 1996 to 2.56% in 1997. Congregational Finances declined from 2.18% in 1996 to 2.15% in 1997. Benevolences measured 0.41% in 1996, and 0.41% in 1997, although the unrounded numbers reflected a slight increase.

In the expanded group of 43 denominations, giving as a percentage of income increased to all three categories. In this expanded set, the percent of income given on a per member basis to Total Contributions grew from 2.64% to 2.65%. Congregational Finances measured 2.21% in both 1996 and 1997, although the unrounded numbers posted a slight increase. Benevolences increased from 0.43% in 1996 to 0.44% in 1997.

The rate of percent change in giving as a percentage of income for the composite group of 29 denominations was -0.75% from the 1996 base for Total Contributions, compared to 0.10% for the expanded group of 43 denominations. For Congregational Finances, the composite group of 29 denominations had a rate of -0.95% change in giving

---

[6] The Church of the Brethren data was being confirmed by the denomination for data years 1996 and 1997. Therefore, that communion is not included in the 1996-1997 analysis, bringing the number of composite denominations to 28 in this analysis.

[7] The denominational giving data considered in this analysis was obtained from the *Yearbook of American and Canadian Churches*, except as noted in the appendices.

**Table 7:** Per Member Giving in 43 Denominations, 1996 and 1997, in Inflation-Adjusted 1992 Dollars and as a Percentage of Income

| Year | Total Contributions Per Member | | Congregational Finances | | Benevolences | |
|---|---|---|---|---|---|---|
| | $s Given in Inflation-Adj. '92 $ | Giving as % of Income | $s Given in Inflation-Adj. '92 $ | Giving as % of Income | $s Given in Inflation-Adj. '92 $ | Giving as % of Income |
| 1996 | $503.32 | 2.64% | $420.66 | 2.21% | $2.67 | 0.43% |
| 1997 | $513.52 | 2.65% | $429.10 | 2.21% | $84.42 | 0.44% |
| Difference from the 1996 Base | $10.20 | 0.01% | $8.44 | 0.00% | $1.76 | 0.01% |
| % Change in Giving as % of Income from the 1996 Base | | 0.10% | | 0.08% | | 0.20% |

Details in the above table may not compute to the numbers shown due to rounding.

as a percentage of income from the 1996 base, compared to 0.08% for the expanded group of 43 denominations. Benevolences for the composite group of 29 denominations had a 0.35% change in giving as a percentage of income from the 1996 base, compared to a rate of 0.20% for the expanded group of 43 denominations.

*Summary.* When the composite data set denominations was expanded to include an additional 15 denominations, bringing the total to 43, approximately ten million additional Full or Confirmed Members were added to the data set. In both the composite denominations set, and the expanded group of 43 denominations, per member giving in inflation-adjusted 1992 dollars increased to

Total Contributions, Congregational Finances and Benevolences from 1996-1997. The expanded group posted larger increases to Total Contributions and Congregational Finances. However, the increase to Benevolences in the expanded group was the same amount as in the composite group of communions.

Per member giving as a percentage of income to Total Contributions and Congregational Finances declined in the composite data set, while it increased in the expanded group of 43 denominations. Both groups posted an increase in per member giving to Benevolences as a percentage of income, although the composite data set showed a slightly larger increase than the expanded set of 43 denominations.

chapter 3
# HIGHLIGHTS

## Church Member Giving in Denominations Defined by Organizational Affiliation, 1968, 1985, and 1997

There is a general operating assumption that members of evangelical churches are "better givers" than are mainline Protestants.

This theory can be tested by comparing giving patterns in two subsets of communions within the composite group of 29 denominations.

Eight of the denominations in the composite data set were affiliated with the National Association of Evangelicals (NAE), a group that, by its choice of name, has identified with the evangelical component of the church.

Seven of the denominations in the composite data set were affiliated with the National Council of the Churches of Christ in the U.S.A. (NCC), a group that traditionally has included what are termed "mainline" denominations.

These fifteen denominations reported data for the years 1968, 1985, and 1997.

In each of these three years, the per member donation was higher in the NAE-affiliated denominations than in the NCC-affiliated denominations.

Both sets of communions exhibited the same patterns in per member contributions in inflation-adjusted dollars. Giving increased from 1968 to 1985, and again from 1985 to 1997 to Total Contributions and Congregational Finances.

Also, both sets of denominations saw increases in per member giving in inflation-adjusted dollars to Benevolences from 1968 to 1985, but decreases between 1985 and 1997.

Figure 6 presents the data for per member contributions in inflation-adjusted 1992 dollars in graphic form for the years 1968, 1985 and 1997.

**Figure 6:** Per Member Giving to Total Contributions, Congregational Finances and Benevolences in Eight NAE and Seven NCC Member Denominations, 1968, 1985 and 1997, Inflation-Adjusted 1992 Dollars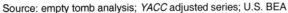

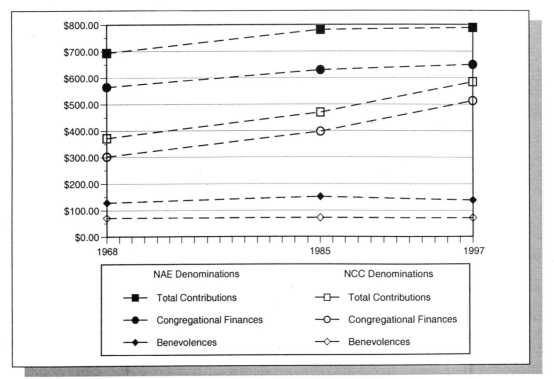

Source: empty tomb analysis; *YACC* adjusted series; U.S. BEA                    empty tomb, inc. 1999

In terms of giving as a percentage of income, both sets of communions declined between 1968 and 1997. Further, the rate of decline between 1985 and 1997 was faster in the NAE-affiliated denominations than in the NCC-affiliated denominations.

In addition, the NCC-affiliated increased in giving as a percentage of income between 1985 and 1997 to the categories of Total Contributions and Congregational Finances.

Figure 7 presents data for giving as a percentage of income to Total Contributions, Congregational Finances and Benevolences for both the NAE and NCC denominations in graphic form for the years 1968, 1985 and 1997.

The NAE-affiliated denominations increased in members by 57% between 1968 and 1997. Therefore, even though these denominations received a smaller portion of income per member, aggregate contributions increased in inflation-adjusted dollars.

**Figure 7:** Per Member Giving as a Percentage of Income to Total Contributions, Congregational Finances and Benevolences, Eight NAE and Seven NCC Denominations, 1968, 1985 and 1997_____

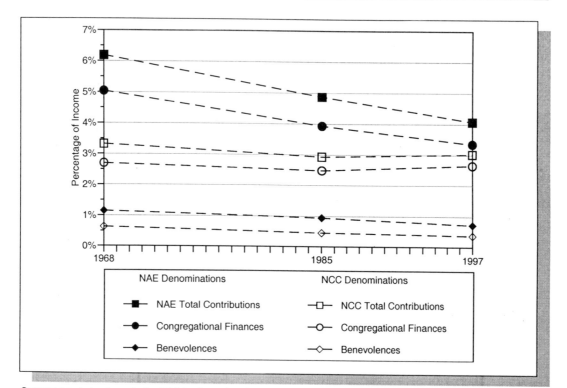

Source: empty tomb analysis; *YACC* adjusted series; U.S. BEA

empty tomb, inc. 1999

The NCC-affiliated denominations declined in members by 27% between 1968 and 1997. Aggregate Benevolences in these denominations decreased by 25% during the 1968-1997 period.

The data suggests that, while members of evangelical churches gave higher amounts to their churches between 1968 and 1997 than did members of mainline churches, the differences in giving patterns between the two groups are shrinking. The negative patterns in giving as a portion of income are evident across the theological spectrum.

# NARRATIVE_____

Although members of evangelical denominations give a higher portion of income than do members of mainline Protestant churches, the rate of decline in total church giving is faster among the evangelicals than in mainline Protestant denominations.

Also, although giving as a percentage of income improved for mainline Protestant denominations from 1985 to 1997, the entire increase was directed to the category of Congregational Finances.

These observations result from a comparison of two subsets of denominations within the larger data set of 29 Protestant communions considered in chapter one of this volume.

In that composite group of 29 denominations, financial data is available for 1968, 1985 and 1997 for eight communions affiliated with the National Association of Evangelicals (NAE).

Seven denominations affiliated with the National Council of the Churches of Christ in the U.S.A. (NCC) also had financial data available for 1968, 1985 and 1997. In the original study that reviewed 1968-1985 data, ten of the denominations included were members of the NCC. Two of these denominations merged in 1987, bringing the number of NCC-affiliated denominations in the larger composite to nine communions. Another denomination in this original grouping indicated it no longer had the staff to compile national financial data after the 1990 data year. That development brought to eight the number of NCC-affiliated denominations with current financial data. This year, one of the eight remaining groups was in the process of obtaining comprehensive Benevolences data for that communion. This denomination had provided data to the *Yearbook of American and Canadian Churches* series since 1921. Efforts are now underway to recover the data that was not collected for 1996 and 1997. It will be included in future editions as it becomes available.

The numbers on the following pages indicate that a decrease in giving as a percentage of income is evident across the theological spectrum. Mainline Protestant churches have already been impacted by the decline in giving. Conversations with staff of some evangelical denominations suggest that they may also begin to feel the effects of a downturn in church member giving. An increasing emphasis on congregational activities aggravated a decline in giving to the category of Benevolences, which includes denominational support.

The analysis in this chapter considers giving in two segments of the church. Of course, there is diversity of opinion within any denomination, as well as in multi-communion groupings such as the NAE or the NCC. For purposes of the present analysis, however, these two groups may serve as general standards for comparison, since they have been characterized as representing certain types of denominations. For example, the National Association of Evangelicals has, by choice of its title, defined its denominational constituency. And traditionally, the National Council of the Churches of Christ in the U.S.A. has counted mainline denominations among its members.

Recognizing that there are limitations in defining a denomination's theological perspectives merely by membership in one of these two organizations, a review of giving patterns of the two subsets of denominations, totaling 15 communions within the larger composite of 29 denominations, may nevertheless provide some insight into how widely spread current giving patterns may be. Therefore, an analysis of 1968-1997 giving patterns was completed for the two subsets of those denominations that were affiliated with one of these two interdenominational organizations.

Using 1985 data, the eight denominations affiliated with the NAE as of 1997 represented 18% of the total number of NAE-member denominations as listed in the Yearbook of American and Canadian *Churches* (*YACC*) series; 21% of the total number of NAE-member denominations with membership data listed in the *YACC*; and approximately 21% of the total membership of the NAE-member denominations with membership data listed in the *YACC*.[8]

Data for 1997 was also available for seven NCC-member denominations in the larger composite group of 29 denominations. In 1985, these seven denominations represented 24% of the total number of NCC constituent bodies as listed in the *YACC*; 27% of the NCC constituent bodies with membership data listed in the *YACC*; and approximately 29% of the total membership of the NCC constituent bodies with membership data listed in the *YACC*.[9]

---

[8] The 1985 total church membership estimate of 3,388,414 represented by NAE denominations includes *YACC* 1985 membership data for each denomination where available or, if 1985 membership data was not available, membership data for the most recent year prior to 1985. Full or Confirmed membership data was used except in those instances where this figure was not available, in which case Inclusive Membership was used.

[9] The 1985 total church membership estimate of 39,621,950 represented by NCC denominations includes *YACC* 1985 membership data for each denomination where available or, if 1985 membership data was not available, membership data for the most recent year prior to 1985. Full or Confirmed membership data was used except in those instances where this figure was not available, in which case Inclusive Membership was used.

**Table 8:** Per Member Giving as a Percentage of Income to Total Contributions for Eight NAE and Seven NCC Denominations, 1968, 1985 and 1997

| Year | NAE Denominations | | | | | NCC Denominations | | | | |
|---|---|---|---|---|---|---|---|---|---|---|
| | Number of Denom. Analyzed | Total Contrib. Per Member as % of Income | Diff. in Total Contrib. Per Member as % of Income from Previous Base | Percent Change in Total Contrib. as % of Income Figured from 1968 Base | Avg. Annual Percent Change in Total Contrib. as % of Income | Number of Denom. Analyzed | Total Contrib. Per Member as % of Income | Diff. in Total Contrib. Per Member as % of Income from Previous Base | Percent Change in Total Contrib. as % of Income Figured from 1968 Base | Avg. Annual Percent Change in Total Contrib. as % of Income |
| 1968 | 8 | 6.19% | | | | 7 | 3.32% | | | |
| 1985 | 8 | 4.87% | -1.32% | -21.26% from '68 | -1.25% | 7 | 2.93% | -0.39% | -11.92% from '68 | -0.70% |
| 1997 | 8 | 4.07% | -0.87% | -13.06% from '85 | -1.09% | 7 | 3.02% | 0.09% | 2.66% from '85 | 0.22% |

Details in the above table may not compute to the numbers shown due to rounding.

***Per Member Giving to Total Contributions, 1968, 1985 and 1997.*** As noted in Table 8, per member giving as a percentage of income to Total Contributions for a composite of those eight NAE-member denominations was 6.19% in 1968. That year, per member giving as a percentage of income to Total Contributions was 3.32% for a composite of these seven NCC denominations.

In 1985, the NAE denominations' per member giving as a percentage of income level was 4.87%, while the NCC level was 2.93%.

The data shows the NAE-member denominations received a larger portion of their members' incomes than did NCC-affiliated denominations in both 1968 and 1985. This information supports the assumption that denominations identifying with an evangelical perspective received a higher level of support than denominations that may be termed mainline.

The analysis also indicates that the decline in levels of giving observed in the larger composite of 29 denominations was evident among both the NAE-member denominations and the NCC-member denominations as well. While giving levels decreased for both sets of denominations between 1968 and 1985, the decrease in Total Contributions was more pronounced in the NAE-affiliated communions. The percent change in the percentage of income donated in the NAE-member denominations, in comparison to the 1968 base, declined 21% between 1968 and 1985, while the percent change in percentage of income given to the NCC-member denominations declined 12%.

Thus, although the evangelical church members continued to give more than mainline church members, the difference in giving levels was smaller in 1985 than in 1968.

A decline in giving as a percentage of income continued among the eight NAE-member denominations during the 1985-1997 period. By 1997, per member giving as a percentage of income to Total Contributions had declined from the 1985 level of 4.87% to 4.07%, a percentage drop of 13% in the portion of members' incomes donated over that eleven-year period.

Meanwhile, the seven NCC-affiliated denominations increased in giving as a percentage of income to Total Contributions during 1985-1997, from the 1985 level of 2.93% to 3.02% in 1997, a percentage increase of 2.66% in the portion of income given to these churches.

Because of the decline in the portion of income given in the NAE-affiliated denominations, in 1997 the difference in per member giving as a percentage of income between the NAE-affiliated denominations and the NCC-affiliated denominations was not as large as it had been in 1968. Comparing the two levels of giving as a percentage of income to Total Contributions between the NAE-member denominations and the NCC-member denominations in this analysis, the NCC-affiliated denominations received 54% as much of per member income as the NAE-member denominations did in 1968, 60% as much in 1985, and 74% in 1997.

For the NAE-affiliated denominations, during the 1985 to 1997 period, the rate of decrease in the average annual percent change in per member giving as a percentage of income to Total Contributions slowed in comparison to the 1968-1985 annual percent change from the 1968 base. The 1968-1985 average annual percent change was -1.25%. The figure for 1985-1997 was -1.09%.

In the NCC-member denominations, the trend reversed. While the average annual percent change from the 1968 base in giving as a percentage of income was -0.70% between 1968 and 1985, the average annual change from 1985 was an increase of 0.22% between 1985 and 1997.

***Per Member Giving to Congregational Finances and Benevolences, 1968, 1985 and 1997.*** Were there any markedly different patterns between the two subsets of denominations defined by affiliation with the NAE and the NCC in regards to the distribution of Total Contributions between the subcategories of Congregational Finances and Benevolences?

In fact, both subsets of communions displayed the same trend noted in the composite group of 29 denominations. In the overall period of 1968 to 1997,

both categories of Congregational Finances and Benevolences declined as a percentage of income in the NCC-affiliated denominations as well as in the NAE-affiliated group. It may be noted, however, that the NCC-related denominations showed an increase in the percentage of income donated to Congregational Finances in the 1985 to 1997 period.

Table 9 presents the Congregational Finances giving data for the NAE and NCC denominations in 1968, 1985 and 1997.

Table 10 presents the Benevolences giving data for the NAE and NCC denominations in 1968, 1985 and 1997.

In 1968, the NAE-affiliated members were giving 6.19% of their incomes to their churches. Of that, 5.04% went to Congregational Finances, while 1.15% went to Benevolences. In 1985, of the 4.87% of income donated to Total Contributions, 3.93% was directed to Congregational Finances. This represented

**Table 9:** Per Member Giving as a Percentage of Income to Congregational Finances in Eight NAE and Seven NCC Denominations, 1968, 1985 and 1997

| | Congregational Finances | | | | | | | | | | |
| | NAE Denominations | | | | | NCC Denominations | | | | | |
| Year | Number of Denom. Analyzed | Cong. Finances Per Member as % of Income | Diff. in Cong. Finances Per Member as % of Income from Previous Base | Percent Change in Cong. Finances as % of Income Figured from 1968 Base | Avg. Annual Percent Change in Cong. Finances as % of Income | Number of Denom. Analyzed | Cong. Finances Per Member as % of Income | Diff. in Cong. Finances Per Member as % of Income from Previous Base | Percent Change in Cong. Finances as % of Income Figured from 1968 Base | Avg. Annual Percent Change in Cong. Finances as % of Income |
|---|---|---|---|---|---|---|---|---|---|---|
| 1968 | 8 | 5.04% | | | | 7 | 2.70% | | | |
| 1985 | 8 | 3.93% | -1.11% | -22.05% from '68 | -1.30% | 7 | 2.48% | -0.22% | -8.09% from '68 | -0.48% |
| 1997 | 8 | 3.35% | -0.58% | -11.49% from '85 | -0.96% | 7 | 2.65% | 0.17% | 6.25% from '85 | 0.52% |

Details in the above table may not compute to the numbers shown due to rounding.

**Table 10:** Per Member Giving as a Percentage of Income to Benevolences in Eight NAE and Seven NCC Denominations, 1968, 1985 and 1997

| | Benevolences | | | | | | | | | | |
| | NAE Denominations | | | | | NCC Denominations | | | | | |
| Year | Number of Denom. Analyzed | Benevol. Per Member as % of Income | Diff. in Benevol. Per Member as % of Income from Previous Base | Percent Change in Benevol. as % of Income Figured from 1968 Base | Avg. Annual Percent Change in Benevol. as % of Income | Number of Denom. Analyzed | Benevol. Per Member as % of Income | Diff. in Benevol. Per Member as % of Income from Previous Base | Percent Change in Benevol. as % of Income Figured from 1968 Base | Avg. Annual Percent Change in Benevol. as % of Income |
|---|---|---|---|---|---|---|---|---|---|---|
| 1968 | 8 | 1.15% | | | | 7 | 0.63% | | | |
| 1985 | 8 | 0.94% | -0.21% | -17.76% from '68 | -1.04% | 7 | 0.45% | -0.18% | -28.36% from '68 | -1.67% |
| 1997 | 8 | 0.72% | -0.22% | -19.96% from '85 | -1.66% | 7 | 0.37% | -0.08% | -12.75% from '85 | -1.06% |

Details in the above table may not compute to the numbers shown due to rounding.

a percent change in the portion of income going to Congregational Finances of -22% from the 1968 base. Per member contributions to Benevolences among these NAE-member denominations declined from 1.15% in 1968 to 0.94% in 1985, representing a percent change of -18% from the 1968 base in the portion of income donated to Benevolences.

In 1997, the 4.07% of income donated by the NAE-member denominations to their churches was divided between Congregational Finances and Benevolences at the 3.35% and 0.72% levels, respectively. The percent change between 1985 and 1997 in contributions to Congregational Finances as a percent of income was a decline of 11%. In contrast, the percent change in contributions to Benevolences as a percent of income was a decline of 20% in the same twelve-year period. The annual rate in the percent change in giving as a percentage of income to Benevolences accelerated to -1.66% between 1985 and 1997, compared to the 1968-1985 rate of -1.04%.

In 1968, the NCC-member denominations were giving 3.32% of their incomes to their churches. Of that, 2.70% went to Congregational Finances. In 1985, of the 2.93% of income donated to these communions, 2.48% went to Congregational Finances. This represented a percent change from the 1968 base in the portion of income going to Congregational Finances of -8%. In contrast, per member contributions as a percent of income to Benevolences among these same NCC-affiliated denominations had declined from 0.63% in 1968 to 0.45% in 1985, representing a percent change of -28% from the 1968 base in the portion of income donated to Benevolences.

In 1997, the 3.02% of income donated by the NCC-affiliated members to their churches was divided between Congregational Finances and Benevolences at the 2.65% and 0.37% levels, respectively. The increase in per member Total Contributions as a percent of income was directed to Congregational Finances, which increased from 2.48% in 1985 to 2.65% in 1997. The 1997 percent change in contributions to Congregational Finances as a percent of income from 1985 was an increase of 6%.

The portion of income directed to Benevolences by these NCC-member denominations declined from 1968 to 1985, and continued to decline from 1985 to 1997. The percent change in contributions to Benevolences as a percent of income declined from 0.45% in 1985 to the 1997 level of 0.37%, a decline of 13% in this eleven-year period. The annual percent change from 1985 in giving as a percentage of income to Benevolences indicated a lower rate of decline at 1.06% between 1985 and 1997, compared to the 1968-1985 annual rate of -1.67%.

***Changes in Per Member Giving, 1968 to 1997.*** For the NAE-affiliated denominations, per member giving as a percentage of income to Congregational Finances declined from 5.04% in 1968 to 3.35% in 1997, a change of -34% from the 1968 base. In Benevolences, the -38% change was due to a decline from 1.15% in 1968 to 0.72% in 1997.

For the NCC-affiliated denominations, between 1968 and 1997, per member giving as a percentage of income declined from 2.70% to 2.65%, a change of -2% in the subcategory of Congregational Finances. That compared to the -41% decline in the subcategory of Benevolences that changed from 0.63% in 1968 to 0.37% in 1997.

Table 11 presents the 1968-1997 percent change in per member giving as a percentage of income to Total Contributions, Congregational Finances and Benevolences in both the NAE- and NCC-affiliated communions.

***Per Member Giving in Inflation-Adjusted 1992 Dollars.*** The NAE-affiliated group level of per member support to Total Contributions in inflation-adjusted 1992 dollars was $693.87 in 1968. This increased to $781.06 in 1985, and increased by 1997 to $788.55.

**Table 11:** Percent Change in Per Member Giving as a Percentage of Income in Eight NAE and Seven NCC Denominations, 1968 to 1997

| Year | NAE Denominations | | | | NCC Denominations | | | |
|---|---|---|---|---|---|---|---|---|
| | Number of Denom. Analyzed | Total Contrib. | Cong. Finances | Benevol. | Number of Denom. Analyzed | Total Contrib. | Cong. Finances | Benevol. |
| 1968 | 8 | 6.19% | 5.04% | 1.15% | 7 | 3.32% | 2.70% | 0.63% |
| 1997 | 8 | 4.07% | 3.35% | 0.72% | 7 | 3.02% | 2.65% | 0.37% |
| % Chg. 1968-97 | 8 | -34% | -34% | -38% | 7 | -9% | -2% | -41% |

Details in the above table may not compute to the numbers shown due to rounding.

For the NAE-affiliated denominations, per member contributions in inflation-adjusted 1992 dollars to the subcategory of Congregational Finances increased from 1968 to 1985, and again from 1985 to 1997. Per member contributions in inflation-adjusted 1992 dollars to Benevolences increased between 1968 and 1985, and decreased between 1985 and 1997.

The NCC-affiliated group experienced an increase in inflation-adjusted per member Total Contributions between 1968 and 1997. The 1968 NCC level of per member support in inflation-adjusted 1992 dollars was $372.73. In 1985, this had increased to $469.31, and in 1997 the figure was $585.20.

The NCC-member denominations experienced an increase in inflation-adjusted per member donations to Congregational Finances in both 1985 and 1997 as well. However, while gifts to Benevolences increased between 1968 and 1985 in inflation-adjusted 1992 dollars, the level of per member contributions to Benevolences decreased between 1985 and 1997.

Thus, in terms of per member giving in inflation-adjusted dollars, the NCC- and NAE-affiliated communions exhibited the same patterns between 1968 and 1997. That is, there was an increase from 1967 to 1985, and again to 1997, in Total Contributions and Congregational Finances, as well as an increase to Benevolences between 1968 and 1985, and a decrease in that category between 1985 and 1997.

As a portion of Total Contributions, the NAE-member denominations directed 19% of their per member gifts to Benevolences in 1968, 19% in 1985, and 18% in 1997. The NCC-member denominations directed 19% of their per member gifts to Benevolences in 1968, 15% in 1985, and 12% in 1997.

Table 12 below presents the levels of per member giving to Total Contributions, Congregational Finances and Benevolences, in inflation-adjusted 1992 dollars, and the percentage of Total Contributions which went to Benevolences in 1968, 1985 and 1997, for both sets of denominations. In addition, the percent change from 1968 to 1997, from the 1968 base, in per member inflation-adjusted 1992 dollar contributions is noted.

***Aggregate Dollar Donations, 1968 and 1997.*** In terms of per member inflation-adjusted 1992 dollar gifts, both the NCC-member churches and the NAE-member denominations posted increases in all three categories, including Benevolences, from 1968 to 1997.

However, a decrease from 1968 to 1997 in per member giving as a percentage of income to all categories among the NAE-member and NCC-member denominations in this analysis suggests that the decline in giving patterns among church members is evident across the theological spectrum. Whatever factors are contributing to this decline, they are not limited to one specific part of the church.

One distinguishing difference between the two subsets of communions was the growth in membership that the evangelical denominations experienced during this period, in contrast to the membership decline reported by the mainline denominations.

While both decreased in per member giving to Benevolences as a percentage of income, the NAE-member denominations grew in membership, and the NCC-member denominations declined in membership. In the NAE-affiliated communions, while members were giving a smaller percentage of income to Benevolences in 1997 than in 1968, the aggregate total dollars available increased. For the NCC-affiliated communions, a decline in per member giving as a percentage of income was coupled with a decrease in membership. Thus, for the NCC-affiliated communions, there was a decrease in aggregate

**Table 12:** Per Member Giving in Eight NAE and Seven NCC Denominations, 1968, 1985 and 1997, Inflation-Adjusted 1992 Dollars

| Year | NAE Denominations | | | | | NCC Denominations | | | | |
|---|---|---|---|---|---|---|---|---|---|---|
| | Number of Denom. Analyzed | Total Contrib. | Cong. Finances | Benevol. | Benevol. as % of Total Contrib. | Number of Denom. Analyzed | Total Contrib. | Cong. Finances | Benevol. | Benevol. as % of Total Contrib. |
| 1968 | 8 | $693.87 | $565.14 | $128.73 | 19% | 7 | $372.73 | $302.25 | $70.48 | 19% |
| 1985 | 8 | $781.06 | $629.72 | $151.34 | 19% | 7 | $469.31 | $397.13 | $72.18 | 15% |
| 1997 | 8 | $788.55 | $649.83 | $138.73 | 18% | 7 | $585.20 | $513.38 | $71.82 | 12% |
| $ Diff. '68-'97 | | $94.68 | $84.68 | $10.00 | | | $212.47 | $211.13 | $1.34 | |
| % Chg. '68-'97 | | 13.6% | 15.0% | 7.8% | | | 57.0% | 69.9% | 1.9% | |

Details in the above table may not compute to the numbers shown due to rounding.

inflation-adjusted Benevolences between 1968 and 1997.

Table 13 considers aggregate giving data for the eight NAE-member denominations included in this study for which data was available for both 1968 and 1997. Membership in these eight NAE-member denominations increased 57% from 1968-1997. Even though per member giving as a percentage of income declined to Total Contributions and the two subcategories of Congregation Finances and Benevolences for the NAE-affiliated denominations, per member giving in inflation-adjusted dollars increased in each of the three categories from 1968 to 1997.

As measured in current dollars, aggregate giving in each of the three categories of Total Contributions, Congregational Finances and Benevolences was greater in 1997 than in 1968 for the NAE-member denominations.

The same can be said for the three aggregate categories when inflation was factored out by converting the current dollars to inflation-adjusted 1992 dollars. These denominations have been compensated for a decline in giving as a percentage of income by the increase in total membership. As long as these denominations continue to grow in membership and maintain constant levels of giving, their national and regional programs may not be affected in the immediate future in the same way some

of the mainline Protestant communions have been impacted by a combination of declining giving and membership.

Table 14 below considers aggregate data for the seven NCC-member denominations. The NCC-related denominations also experienced an increase in aggregate current dollars in each of the three categories of Total Contributions, Congregational Finances and Benevolences, even with a posted decline in membership.

However, the inflation-adjusted 1992 dollar figures account for the acknowledged financial difficulties in many of these communions, particularly in the category of Benevolences. The decline in membership affected the total income received by this group of denominations. Between 1968 and 1997, while the NCC-related communions experienced an increase of 57% in per member giving to Total Contributions in inflation-adjusted 1992 dollars—from $372.73 in 1968 to $585.20 in 1997—aggregate Total Contributions in 1997 to these eight denominations was only 15% larger in inflation-adjusted 1992 dollars in 1997 than in 1968.

In regard to the two categories of Congregational Finances and Benevolences, Congregational Finances absorbed the increased giving. The -25% decline in aggregated Benevolences receipts in inflation-adjusted 1992 dollars between 1968 and 1997 provides insight into the basis for any cutbacks at the denominational level.

**Table 13:** Aggregate Giving, Eight NAE Denominations, 1968 and 1997, in Current and Inflation-Adjusted 1992 Dollars

| Year | Number of Den. Analyzed | Member-ship | Current Dollars | | | Inflation-Adjusted 1992 Dollars | | |
|---|---|---|---|---|---|---|---|---|
| | | | Total Contributions | Cong. Finances | Benevol. | Total Contributions | Cong. Finances | Benevol. |
| 1968 | 8 | 535,865 | $102,845,802 | $83,765,677 | $19,080,125 | $371,821,410 | $302,840,481 | $68,980,929 |
| 1997 | 8 | 841,827 | $740,299,059 | $610,059,729 | $130,239,330 | $663,826,272 | $547,040,647 | $116,785,626 |
| % Chg. | | 57% | 620% | 628% | 583% | 79% | 81% | 69% |

Details in the above table may not compute to the numbers shown due to rounding.

**Table 14:** Aggregate Giving, Seven NCC Denominations, 1968 and 1997, in Current and Inflation-Adjusted 1992 Dollars

| Year | Number of Den. Analyzed | Member-ship | Current Dollars | | | Inflation-Adjusted 1992 Dollars | | |
|---|---|---|---|---|---|---|---|---|
| | | | Total Contributions | Cong. Finances | Benevol. | Total Contributions | Cong. Finances | Benevol. |
| 1968 | 7 | 12,688,864 | $1,308,180,158 | $1,060,822,881 | $247,357,277 | $4,729,501,656 | $3,835,223,720 | $894,277,936 |
| 1997 | 7 | 9,321,281 | $6,083,208,043 | $5,336,629,413 | $746,578,630 | $5,454,813,525 | $4,785,356,360 | $669,457,165 |
| % Chg. | | -27% | 365% | 403% | 202% | 15% | 25% | -25% |

Details in the above table may not compute to the numbers shown due to rounding.

***Summary.*** An analysis of giving as a percentage of income found a negative trend between 1968 and 1997 in the portion of income given by church members across the theological spectrum. Denominations affiliated with both the NAE and the NCC were receiving a lower level of giving as a percentage of income on a per member basis.

On one hand, the NAE-member denominations received a higher portion of income on a per member basis than did the NCC-member denominations throughout this period. On the other hand, between 1968 and 1985, the NAE-member denominations experienced a higher rate of decrease in average annual percent change in giving as a percentage of income, from the 1968 base, in the categories of Total Contributions and Congregational Finances than did the NCC-member denominations. In the category of Benevolences, between 1968 and 1985, the NCC-member denominations had a higher rate of decrease in average annual percent change in giving as a percentage of income from the 1968 base than did the NAE-member denominations.

Between 1985 and 1997, the NAE-member denominations experienced a higher rate of decrease in average annual percent change in per member giving as a percentage of income from the 1985 base than did the NCC-member denominations in each of the three categories of Total Contributions, Congregational Finances and Benevolences. Further, in the category of Congregational Finances, the NCC-member denominations increased from 1985 to 1997.

In the NAE-member denominations, the rate of decrease in per member giving as a percentage of income to Benevolences quickened during the 1985-1997 period compared to the 1968-1985 period. In the NCC-member denominations, the rate of decrease in per member giving as a percentage of income to Benevolences slowed between 1985-1997, compared to 1968-1985.

After inflation was factored out by converting the data to inflation-adjusted 1992 dollars, both the NAE-affiliated and the NCC-affiliated denominations received more dollars per member for the categories of Total Contributions, Congregational Finances, and Benevolences, in 1997 than in 1968.

The NAE-affiliated denominations were growing in membership during the 1968-1997 period. As a result, aggregate income to these denominations also increased. In the NCC-affiliated denominations experienced a decline in membership. The result was a decrease in aggregate Benevolences for the NCC-member denominations between 1968 and 1997 in inflation-adjusted dollars.

The generally-held belief that evangelicals were "better givers" than mainline members is correct in that per member giving was higher in the NAE-affiliated denominations both in terms of giving as a percentage of income and inflation-adjusted contributions when compared to NCC-member denominations throughout the 1968 to 1997 period.

However, the rate of decline in per member giving as a percentage of income between 1985 and 1997 was more pronounced among the NAE-affiliated denominations than among the NCC-affiliated denominations for the three categories of Total Contributions, Congregational Finances, and Benevolences.

The negative direction in per member giving as a percentage of income over the 30-year time span under review in both the NAE-affiliated and NCC-affiliated denominations suggests that the negative trend in giving patterns is not limited to a particular portion of the theological spectrum.

chapter 4
# HIGHLIGHTS

*Church Member Giving*
*in Eleven Denominations,*
*1921-1997*

Data over an extended period of time is available in the *Yearbook of American and Canadian Churches* series for a group of 11 Protestant communions, or their historical antecedents. This set includes ten mainline Protestant communions and the Southern Baptist Convention.

In 1921, per member giving as a percentage of income was 2.9%. From 1922 through 1933, giving as a portion of income stayed above the 3% level. In 1933, the depth of the Great Depression, giving was 3.3%. However, as the Depression continued, the increases in giving did not keep up with recovering incomes. Therefore, the percentage of income given declined.

Incomes continued to increase faster than giving during World War II. As a consequence, giving declined to 2.0% in 1945.

During the 1950s, the amount of income given recovered to pre-Depression levels, reaching and then staying above 3% from 1958 through 1963. As it had in the 1920s, during the 1950s giving increased even as incomes went up.

However, the rate of giving increases began to decline in the period from 1960-1964. This period predates many of the controversies that were later given as reasons for declines in giving.

In 1968, giving was at the 2.7% level. By 1985, it measured 2.45% of income, and in 1997, it had moved up to 2.47%.

The data indicates that per member giving as a percentage of income was lower in 1997 than in either 1921 or 1933.

Figure 8 contrasts per member giving as a percentage of income for a composite of eleven Protestant denominations, with U.S. disposable personal income in inflation-adjusted 1992 dollars, for the period 1921 through 1997.

**Figure 8:** Per Member Giving as a Percentage of Income in 11 Denominations, and U.S. Per Capita Income 1921-1997 _____

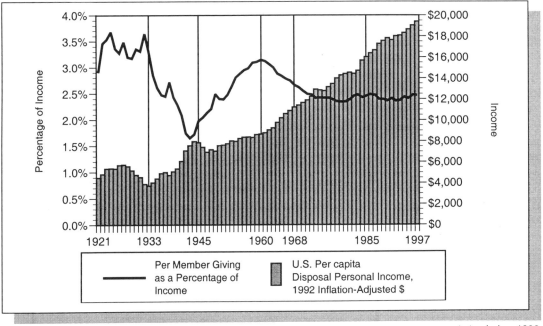

Source: empty tomb analysis; *YACC* adjusted series; U.S. BEA                    empty tomb, inc. 1999

## NARRATIVE_____

A continuing feature in this ongoing series reviewing church member giving is an analysis of available giving data throughout this century. The data can now be updated to include information through 1997. Also, efforts are regularly made to improve the data set. For example, this year information for several years was refined by one denomination. Therefore, this analysis is again presented, this year with the most complete information available through 1997.

For the period 1921 through 1997, comparable data since 1921 is not readily available for all 29 communions in the composite analysis. However, data over an extended period of time is available in the *Yearbook of American and Canadian Churches* series for a group of 11 Protestant communions, or their historical antecedents. This set includes ten mainline Protestant communions and the Southern Baptist Convention.

The available data has been reported fairly consistently over the time span of 1921 to 1997.[10] The value of the multiyear comparison is that it provides a historical time line over which to observe giving patterns.

***Giving as a Percentage of Income.*** The period under consideration in this section of the report began in 1921. At that point, per member giving as a percentage of income was 2.9%. In current dollars, U.S. per capita disposable (after-tax) personal income was $555, and per member giving was $16. When inflation was factored out by converting both income and giving to 1992 dollars, per capita income in 1921 measured $4,479 and per member giving was $130.

From 1922 through 1933, giving as a percent of income stayed above the 3% level. The high was 3.68% in 1924, followed closely by the amount in 1932, when per member giving measured 3.65% of per capita income. This trend is of particular interest inasmuch as per capita income was increasing steadily between 1921 and 1927, with the exception of a decline in 1925. Even as people were increasing in personal affluence, they also continued to maintain a giving level of more than 3% to their churches. When income began to decline because of the economic reverses in the Great Depression, giving continued to measure above 3% from 1929 through 1933.

The year 1933 was the depth of the Great Depression. Per capita income was at the lowest point it would reach between 1921 and 1997, whether measured in current or inflation-adjusted dollars. Yet per member giving as a percentage of income was 3.3%. Income had decreased by 17% between 1921 and 1933 in inflation-adjusted 1992 dollars, from $4,479 to $3,727. Meanwhile, per member giving had decreased 6%, from $130 in 1921 to $123 in 1933, in inflation-adjusted dollars. Therefore, giving as a percentage of income actually increased from 2.9% in 1921 to 3.3% in 1933, an increase of 13% in the portion of income contributed to the church.

Giving in inflation-adjusted 1992 dollars declined from 1933 to 1934, although income began to recover in 1934. Giving then began to increase again in 1935. In inflation-adjusted dollars, giving did not return to the 1927 level of $200 until 1953, when giving grew from $192 in 1952 to $211 in 1953.

During World War II, incomes improved rapidly. Meanwhile, church member giving increased only modestly in current dollars. When inflation was factored out, per member giving was at $126.61 in 1941, the year the United States entered the war. It declined to $123.24 in 1942, increased in 1943 to $124.73, and then to $136.98 in 1944. However, income in inflation-adjusted dollars grew from $6,061 in 1941 to $7,061 in 1942, $7,542 in 1943, and reached a high for this period of $7,949 in 1944, a level that would not be surpassed again until 1953. Thus, giving as a percentage of income reached a low point of 1.7% during 1942, 1943 and 1944, the three full calendar years of formal U.S. involvement in World War II.

In 1945, the last year of the war, U.S. per capita income was $7,850 in inflation-adjusted dollars. Giving in inflation-adjusted dollars was $155 that year. Although per member giving increased 26% between 1933 and 1945, per capita income had increased 111%. Giving as a percentage of income therefore declined from the 3.3% level in 1933, to 2.0% in 1945.

The unusually high level of per capita income slumped after the war but had recovered to war levels by the early 1950s. By 1960, U.S. per capita income was 10% higher in inflation-adjusted 1992 dollars than it had been in 1945, increasing from $7,850 in 1945 to $8,647 in 1960. Meanwhile, per member giving in inflation-adjusted dollars had increased 75%, from $155 in 1945 to $272 in 1960. Giving recovered the level it had been from 1922 through 1933, and stayed above 3% from 1958 through 1963. Giving as a percentage of income reached a postwar high of 3.15% in 1960, and then began to decline.

For the second time in the century, giving levels were growing to, or maintaining a level above, three percent of income even while incomes were also expanding. From 1921-1928, incomes expanded 24%. During this time giving grew to above 3% and stayed there. From 1950-1963, incomes grew 22%. Again, giving grew to above 3% and stayed there. In both cases, church members increased or maintained their giving levels even as their incomes increased.

---

[10] Data for the period 1965-1967 was not available in a form that could be readily analyzed for the present purposes, and therefore data for these three years was estimated by dividing the change in per member current dollar contributions from 1964 to 1968 by four, the number of years in this interval, and cumulatively adding the result to the base year of 1964 data and subsequently to the calculated data for the succeeding years of 1965 and 1966 in order to obtain estimates for the years 1965-1967.

In the 1920s, the economic expansion was interrupted by the Great Depression, followed by World War II.

In contrast to the economic upheaval earlier in the century, however, the economy continued to expand through the 1960s. Yet the portion of income given was not sustained above 3%. By 1968, giving as a percentage of income had declined to 2.7% for this group of 11 communions. U.S. per capita income increased 30% in inflation-adjusted 1992 dollars between 1960 and 1968, from $8,647 in 1960 to $11,211 in 1968. In comparison, per member giving increased 10% in inflation-adjusted dollars, from the 1960 level of $272 to the 1968 level of $299.

By 1985, per member giving had increased 32% in inflation-adjusted 1992 dollars, from $299 in 1968 to $393 in 1985. U.S. per capita income measured $16,026, an increase of 43% over the 1968 level of $11,211. Giving as a percentage of income, therefore, measured 2.45% in 1985.

The year 1997 was the latest year for which data was available for the eleven denominations considered in this section. In that year, per member giving as a percentage of income was 2.47%, an increase from the 1985 level of 2.45%. Per member giving had increased 22% in inflation-adjusted 1992 dollars, from $393 in 1985 to $480 in 1997. U.S. per capita income had increased 21% during this period, from the 1985 level of $16,026 to the 1997 level of $19,398. Thus, the percentage of income donated increased slightly.

***Change in Per Member Giving and U.S. Per Capita Disposable Personal Income, in Inflation-adjusted 1992 Dollars.*** For this group of 11 communions, per member giving in inflation-adjusted 1992 dollars increased half the time during the 1921-1947 period. Per member giving in inflation-adjusted dollars decreased from 1924 to 1925. While it increased from 1925 to 1926 and again in 1927, giving began a seven-year decline in 1928. This seven-year period, from 1928 to 1934, included some of the worst years of the Great Depression. Giving increased again in 1935. Declines in 1939, 1940, 1942, 1946 and 1947 alternated with increases in the other years.

Then, from 1948 through 1969,[11] these 11 communions increased in per member giving in inflation-adjusted 1992 dollars. Further, the period from 1948 to the year 1960, when giving as a percentage of income reached its postwar peak, posted the highest prolonged annual increase in per member giving in inflation-adjusted dollars during this 1921-1997 period of 77 years. During the 1948-1960 interval of 12 years, per member giving averaged an increase of $9.47 a year. Although giving continued to increase for the next few years from 1960 to 1969, it was at the slower rate of $2.94 per year.

Per member giving in inflation-adjusted dollars declined in 1970 and 1971, followed by two years of increase and two of decline.

There was also a sustained increase during the 21-year interval of 1976-1997. During this interval, income increased an average of $315.01 annually in inflation-adjusted 1992 dollars. Meanwhile, per member giving increased $7.72 on average each year, a higher overall rate than during the 21-year interval of 1948-1969, when the annual increase was $6.67. Giving increased 51% from 1976 to 1997, while income increased 48%. Therefore, giving as a percentage of income was 2.42% in 1976 and 2.47% in 1997.

By reviewing this data in smaller increments of years from 1950 to 1997, as presented in Table 15, the time period in which giving began to decline markedly can be identified.

As indicated in Table 15, during the 1950 to 1997 period, the highest annual increase in per member giving in inflation-adjusted 1992 dollars occurred from 1950-1955. In terms of the highest annual increase in giving as a percentage of the annual change in U.S. per capita income, that period was the years 1955 to 1960. During 1980 to 1985, a higher average per member annual dollar increase of $11.07 was given, compared to the $6.91 donated in 1955-1960. However, the larger amount of $11.07 represented only 3.42% of the average annual increase in U.S. per capita income, compared to the 8.51% which the $6.91 represented during 1955 to 1960. The $8.25 in the 1990-1997 period also represented a higher portion of the average annual increase in income than that of the 1980-1985 period.

Giving declined markedly between 1960 and 1964 in these communions. While income was increasing at an annual rate of $277 in this four-year period, 241% greater than in the 1955-1960 period, the average annual increase in per member contributions in inflation-adjusted 1992 dollars was $2.29, 67% smaller in 1960-1964 than it was in 1955-1960.

---

[11] Excluding the years 1965 through 1967 for which estimated data is used. See first footnote in this chapter.

**Table 15:** Average Annual Increase in U.S. Per Capita Income and Per Member Giving in 11 Denominations, 1950-1997, Inflation-adjusted 1992 Dollars

| Time Period | U.S. Per Capita Income | | | Per Member Giving | | | Avg. Ann. Chg. Giv. as % Avg. Ann. Chg. Income |
|---|---|---|---|---|---|---|---|
| | First Year in Period | Last Year in Period | Average Annual Change | First Year in Period | Last Year in Period | Average Annual Change | |
| 1950-1955 | $7,556 | $8,241 | $136.98 | $181.36 | $237.61 | $11.25 | 8.21% |
| 1955-1960 | $8,241 | $8,647 | $81.19 | $237.61 | $272.14 | $6.91 | 8.51% |
| 1960-1964[12] | $8,647 | $9,755 | $277.02 | $272.14 | $281.30 | $2.29 | 0.83% |
| 1964-1970[12] | $9,755 | $11,639 | $314.06 | $281.00 | $296.61 | $2.55 | 0.81% |
| 1970-1975 | $11,639 | $12,783 | $228.77 | $296.61 | $309.32 | $2.54 | 1.11% |
| 1975-1980 | $12,783 | $14,409 | $325.07 | $309.32 | $337.96 | $5.73 | 1.76% |
| 1980-1985 | $14,409 | $16,026 | $323.58 | $337.96 | $393.31 | $11.07 | 3.42% |
| 1985-1990 | $16,026 | $17,824 | $359.59 | $393.31 | $422.13 | $5.76 | 1.60% |
| 1990-1997 | $17,824 | $19,398 | $224.84 | $422.13 | $479.87 | $8.25 | 3.67% |

Details in the above table may not compute to the numbers shown due to rounding.

The 1960-1964 period predates many of the controversial issues often cited as reasons for declining giving. Also, it was at the end of the 1960-1964 period when membership began to decrease in mainline denominations, ten of which are included in this group. Therefore, additional exploration of that period of time might be merited.

Increases in per member giving were consistently low from 1960-1975. The annual rates of increase of $2.29 per year from 1960 to 1964, $2.55 from 1964 to 1970, and $2.54 from 1970 to 1975, were the lowest in the 1950 to 1997 period. Throughout the 1960 to 1970 period, the increase in dollars given represented less than one percent of the average annual increase in per capita income, while from 1970-1975, it was 1.11%.

In the 1975-1980 period, the average annual increase in giving increased to $5.73, representing 1.76% of the average annual increase in per capita income.

From 1980 to 1985, the average annual increase in giving rose to $11.07. This amount of $11.07—representing 3.42% of the average annual increase in income during the 1980-1985 period—was the second highest average annual rate of increase in terms of per member giving in inflation-adjusted dollars during the 1950 to 1997 period. As a portion of the increase in per capita income, the 3.42% of the 1980 to 1985 period was the fourth largest annual rate of increase in the 1950 to 1997 period.

The annual average increase in giving as a percent of the average annual income increase during 1985 to 1990 fell from the 1980 to 1985 period. The average annual rate of change increased in the seven-year period from 1990 to 1997. The rate increased both in terms of change in per member giving in inflation-adjusted dollars, and as a percent of the average annual income increase.

***Per Member Giving as Percentage of Income, 1921, 1933 and 1997.*** By 1997, U.S. per capita disposable (after-tax) personal income had increased 333%, in inflation-adjusted 1992 dollars, since 1921, and 420% since 1933—the depth of the Great Depression.

Meanwhile, by 1997, per member giving in inflation-adjusted 1992 dollars had increased 269% since 1921, and 291% since the depth of the Great Depression.

Consequently, per member giving as a percentage of income was lower in 1997 than in either 1921 or 1933. In 1921, per member giving as a percentage of income was 2.9%. In 1933, it was 3.3%. In 1997, per member giving as a percentage of income was 2.5% for the composite of the eleven denominations considered in this section. Thus, the percent change in the per member portion of income donated to the church had declined by 15% from the 1921 base, from 2.9% in 1921 to 2.5% in 1997, and by 25% from the 1933 base, from 3.3% in 1933 to 2.5% in 1997.

---

[12] See the first footnote in this chapter for an explanation of the selection of 1960-1964 and 1964-1970, rather than 1960-1965 and 1965-1970.

Appendix A contains a listing of the denominations contained in this analysis.

***Summary.*** For a group of 11 Protestant denominations, giving as a percentage of income was above 3% of U.S. per capita disposable personal income from 1922 through 1933. It dropped below 3% in the later part of the Great Depression and reached a low point during World War II. The level of giving improved until, from 1958 through 1963, it recovered to the levels evident earlier in the century, maintaining at more than 3%. The post-war high was reached in 1960, after which giving began to decline as a portion of income.

During the years 1921-1997, two 21-year periods posted increases in per member giving in inflation-adjusted 1992 dollars. Per member giving during the years 1947 to 1969 increased by an annual average of $6.67. During 1976-1997, the annual average increase was $7.72. However, between 1948 and 1960, per member giving increased at an annual average rate of $9.47.

Per member giving and U.S. per capita disposable personal income, both in inflation-adjusted 1992 dollars, were analyzed in smaller increments for the years 1950-1997. The data indicates there was a marked decline in the rate of giving increase in the 1960-1964 period.

The data also indicates that giving as a portion of income was higher in both 1921 and 1933 than in 1997.

*Church Member Giving*
*and Membership Trends*
*Based on 1968-1997 Data*

According to a study released in late 1999, the planet Earth is in for a tough time.

A model keyed to data for 1850—predating the effects of the industrial revolution—suggests that global warming will so heat the planet in the next century that world food production will be threatened. Because the world's forests will be adversely affected, the entire ecosystem will be in trouble.

The Hadley Center for Climate Change in Berkshire, England, released the report at an international conference. The preliminary results from the model show more serious conditions than previously anticipated. Therefore, the scientists wanted to release the report as soon as possible.[13]

By releasing the report, one may conclude, the scientists hoped that people in authority will evaluate the information in a timely fashion. Even better, these leaders may take corrective action, particularly to preserve the forests and thus intervene in a destructive cycle.

Statistical regression models are a tool to help leaders plan. Communities use them to know whether to build schools and roads. Hospitals consider trends to know the direction of health care in the next century.

_____

[13] Paul Brown, "Century of Natural Disasters Predicted," an article from *The Guardian*, appearing in *The* (Champaign, Ill.) *News-Gazette*, November 14, 1999, B-1, cols. 1-4.

Trends can also be useful to church leaders. Present behavior may change through education efforts, or a change in spirituality. But what if it does not? What conditions face the church in the future if present patterns continue?

The authors of this volume first began looking at trends in response to conversations with various denominational leaders. The current giving data was reflecting conditions that produced serious consequences. Some denominations were cutting back on programs and staff. Leaders were making painful decisions about congregational priorities. What would happen if the present trends continued?

Data is available for both giving and membership. The Narrative section describes the standard statistical procedures used in the analyses.

***Trends in Giving as a Percentage of Income.*** Giving as a percentage of income to both Congregational Finances and Benevolences indicate negative trends between 1968 and 1997. That data can be extended to consider what would happen to giving levels if these trends continued in an uninterrupted fashion.

At present rates, giving to Congregational Finances will represent 1.4% of income in 2050, down 35% from the 1997 level.

Giving to Benevolences will be 0.2% of income in 2050, down 50% from 0.4% in 1997. Based on available data, it is not clear if exponential regression or linear regression better describes the trend in per member giving to Benevolences. If linear regression is the better descriptor, then congregations will have ceased to spend any money beyond themselves by the middle of the next century.

***Trends in Membership.*** Membership data suggests that the church is shrinking as a percentage of population in the U.S.

Eleven mainline Protestant denominations represented 13% of the population in 1968, and 7.6% in 1997. At these rates, this group will include 2.9% of the population in the year 2050, a decline of 62% from the 1997 level.

The composite data set communions were 14.1% of the population in 1968 and 11.5% in 1997. The trends suggest that this group will be 7.6% of the population in 2050.

See Figure 9 for a graphic presentation of membership as a percentage of U.S. population and giving as a percentage of income for the composite denominations from 1968 to 1997.

**Figure 9:** Giving as a Percentage of Income and Membership as a Percentage of U.S. Population, Composite Denominations, 1968-1997_____

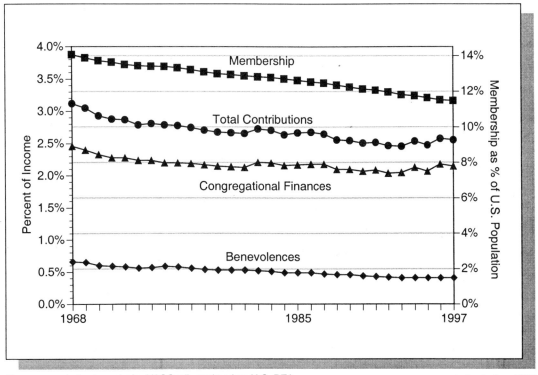

Source: empty tomb analysis; *YACC* adjusted series; U.S. BEA          empty tomb, inc. 1999

Membership data is also available for seven additional Protestant denominations, including some of the faster growing denominations in the country, and the Roman Catholic Church. This larger set of denominations represented 45% of the U.S. population in 1968, and 39% in 1997, a decline of 12% from the 1968 base.

Trend data only indicates future directions. Data does not dictate what will happen. Church leaders and members can decide what the future will look like. Available information, including trend analysis, can help formulate intelligent responses to current trends.

## NARRATIVE_____

Statistical analyses help concerned leaders address issues that will affect the quality of life for future generations 25 or 100 years from now.

Statistical techniques can also be used to suggest both consequences and possibilities regarding church giving and membership patterns as well. This type of trend analysis is useful in considering what data suggests the future will look like if the patterns of the past three decades continue in an uninterrupted fashion.

*The Meaning of Trends.* Linear regression and exponential regression are both standard statistical techniques that can be used to provide trend projections. The results of such analyses should be evaluated with the realization that these types of projections indicate—rather than dictate—future directions. For example, in the present church member giving analysis, the data can be used to develop giving trends that suggest what giving will look like in coming decades. These trends indicate the present general direction of giving. Various factors—such as intentional education efforts by congregations and/or denominations, or spiritual renewal, or a decided loss of commitment to the church—could change giving patterns in unforeseen ways, either positively or negatively. Trends, therefore, are based on the assumption that either current conditions will remain constant, or present suppositions regarding the future are valid. The trends point out the future of giving, if patterns continue without interruption. With those considerations in mind, one may explore what implications present data patterns have for the future.

This analysis was first conducted, in part, as a result of present church conditions. After talking with numerous denominational officials who were making painful decisions about which programs to cut, in light of decreased Benevolences dollars being received, it seemed useful to see where the present patterns of giving might lead if effective means were not found to alter present behavior. Were current patterns likely to prove a temporary setback, or did the data suggest longer-term implications?

***The Current Trend in Church Giving.*** The first chapter in this report indicates that per member giving as a percentage of income has been decreasing over a 30-year period. Further, contributions to the category of Benevolences have been declining proportionately faster than those to Congregational Finances between 1968 and 1997.

The data for the composite denominations analyzed for 1968 through 1997 has been projected in *The State of Church Giving* series, beginning with the edition that included 1991 data.[14] The most recent projection is based on data from 1968 through 1997.

The data for both Benevolences and Congregational Finances can be projected using linear and exponential regression analysis. To determine

which type of analysis more accurately describes the data in a category's giving patterns, the data for 1968-1985 was projected using both techniques. Then, the actual data for 1986 through 1997 was plotted. The more accurate projection was judged to be the procedure that produced the trend line most closely resembling the actual 1986-1997 data.

***The Trend in Congregational Finances.*** The 1968-1997 church giving data contained in this report indicates that giving as a percentage of income for Congregational Finances declined from 2.46% in 1968, to 2.15% in 1997, a decline of 12%.

Both linear and exponential regression were used to analyze the data for giving as a percentage of income to Congregational Finances for the 17-year interval of 1968 through 1985. Then the actual data for 1986 through 1997 was plotted. The results are shown in Figure 10.

In the case of giving as a percentage of income to Congregational Finances, the actual data for 1986-1997 was at or above the exponential curve. The exponential curve suggests that by the year 2050, giving to Congregational Finances will be at 1.40%, down from 2.15% in 1997, a decrease of 35% in the portion of income donated to support the activities of the congregations.

***The Trend in Benevolences.*** Of the two subcategories within Total Contributions, that is, Congregational Finances and Benevolences, the more pronounced negative trend occurred in Benevolences. Between 1968 and 1997, per member contributions to Benevolences as a percentage of income decreased from 0.66% in 1968 to 0.41% in 1997, a percent change in giving as a percentage of income of -38% from the 1968 base.

The data for giving as a percentage of income to Benevolences for the 17-year interval of 1968 through 1985 was also projected using both linear and exponential regression. The actual data for 1986 through 1997 was then plotted. The results are shown in Figure 11.

Through 1995, the linear trend corresponded more closely to the actual data for giving as a percentage of income to Benevolences. Per member giving as a percentage of income to Benevolences mea-

[14] John Ronsvalle and Sylvia Ronsvalle, *The State of Church Giving through 1991* (Champaign, IL: empty tomb, inc., 1993), and subsequent editions in the series. The edition with data through 1991 provides a discussion of the choice to use giving as a percentage of income as a basis for considering future giving patterns.

**Figure 10:** Projected Trends for Composite Denominations, Giving as a Percentage of Income to Congregational Finances, Using Linear and Exponential Regression Based on Data for 1968-1985, with Actual Data for 1986-1997

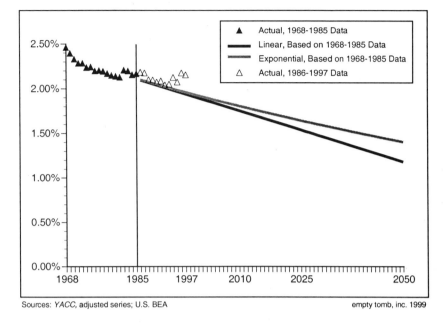

Sources: *YACC*, adjusted series; U.S. BEA

empty tomb, inc. 1999

**Figure 11:** Projected Trends for Composite Denominations, Giving as a Percentage of Income to Benevolences, Using Linear and Exponential Regression Based on Data for 1968-1985, with Actual Data for 1986-1997

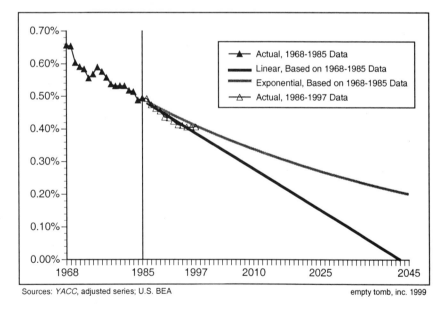

Sources: *YACC*, adjusted series; U.S. BEA

empty tomb, inc. 1999

sured below the linear trend line in five out of six years from 1989 through 1994. However, it measured above the linear trend line for 1995 through 1997. Nevertheless, the reported data for these years continued to be lower than the exponential trend line. As a result, only future data will indicate which trend best describes long-term giving to Benevolences.

In the meantime, a range of giving levels can be presented. If the giving patterns of the past 30 years continue in an uninterrupted fashion, then per member giving as a portion of income to the category of Benevolences will reach 0% of income in the year A.D. 2044, if the linear trend is more accurate. If the exponential curve proves to be more descriptive, giving in 2044 would be 0.20%, down 50% from the 0.41% level in 1997.[15] In both trend lines, by 2044 the amount of income going to support Benevolences, including denominational structures, would be

---

[15] In the linear regression, the value for the correlation coefficient, or $r_{XY}$, for the Benevolences data is -.98. The strength of the linear relationship in the present set of 1968-1997 data, that is, the proportion of variance accounted for by linear regression, is represented by the coefficient of determination, or $r^2_{XY}$, of .97 for Benevolences. In the exponential regression, the value for the $r_{XY}$, for the Benevolences data is -.99, while the strength of the exponential relationship is also .97. The Benevolences F-observed values of 844.82 for the linear, and 1,008.03 for the curvilinear, regression are substantially greater than the F-critical value of 7.64 for 1 and 28 degrees of freedom for a single-tailed test with an Alpha value of 0.01. Therefore, the regression equation is useful at the level suggested by the $r^2_{XY}$ figure in predicting giving as a percentage of income.

either negligible or severely reduced, if current patterns hold constant.

***Membership in the Composite Denominations, 1968-1997.*** Earlier chapters discuss the patterns in church member giving data for a composite set of denominations. In addition to giving patterns, how does membership for this group fare?

This group of denominations, which span the theological spectrum, included 28,219,613 Full or Confirmed Members in 1968. By 1997, these communions included 30,765,797 members, an increase of 9%.[16] However, during the same 30-year period, U.S. population had increased from 200,745,000 to 267,880,000, an increase of 33%. Therefore, while this grouping represented 14% of the U.S. population in 1968, it included 11% in 1997.

***Trends in Church Membership as a Percentage of U.S. Population.[17]*** *The State of Church Giving through 1993* includes a chapter entitled, "A Unified Theory of Giving and Membership." The hypothesis explored in that discussion is that there is a relationship between a decline in church member giving and membership patterns. One proposal considered in that chapter is that a denomination which is able to involve its members in a larger vision as evidenced in giving patterns will also be attracting additional members.

In the present edition, discussion will be limited to patterns and trends in membership as a percentage of U.S. population.

***Membership in Eleven Mainline Denominations.*** The declining membership trends have been noticed most markedly in the mainline Protestant communions. Full or Confirmed Membership in eleven mainline Protestant denominations affiliated with the National Council of

the Churches of Christ in the U.S.A.[18] decreased as a percentage of U.S. population by 42% between 1968 and 1997. In 1968, this group included 26,452,819, or 13.2% of U. S. population. In 1997, the group included 20,451,595, or 7.6% of U.S. population.

As with giving as a percentage of income to Congregational Finances and Benevolences, trend lines using both linear and exponential regression were developed for these eleven mainline Protestant communions, using their 1968-1985 membership data. The actual 1986 through 1997 data was also plotted. As shown in Figure 12, the actual 1986-1997 data more closely follows the exponential curve. The data would therefore suggest that these eleven denominations will represent 2.9% of the U.S. population by the year 2050, a decrease of 62% from the 1997 level of 7.6%.

***Membership Trends in the Composite Denominations.*** Nine of the eleven mainline Protestant denominations discussed above are included in the composite denominations that have been considered in earlier chapters of this report. Regression analysis was carried out on the 1968-1985 data for the composite denominations to determine if the trends in the larger grouping differed from the mainline denomination subset. The results were then compared to the actual 1986 through 1997 membership data for the composite data set.

The composite denominations represented 14.1% of the U.S. population in 1968, and 12.6% in 1985. Linear trend analysis suggests that this grouping would have represented 11.66% of U.S. population in 1997, while exponential regression suggests it would have been 11.75%. In fact, this composite grouping of communions represented 11.48% of the U.S.

---

[16] Of the 30 denominations in the composite data set considered in earlier chapters, financial information was not available for the Friends United Meeting after 1990. Therefore, the composite was referred to as a set of 29 denominations. This was true even though the Church of the Brethren, one of the 29, did not provide complete 1996 or 1997 financial data in time for the current report. As of this edition, inclusive membership for the Friends United Meeting was obtained for 1991 through 1997. Therefore, in this chapter, the composite set of denominations generally refers to a set of 29 denominations regarding financial data (actually 28 for 1996 and 1997), and 30 denominations for membership analysis. See Appendix B-1 for details. Consult Appendix B-4 for the Total Membership numbers used for the American Baptist Churches in the U.S.A. See Appendix

B-3.3 and Appendix B-4 for the membership data of the other denominations included in subsequent analyses in this chapter that are not one of the composite denominations.

[17] The denominations analyzed in this section include the composite of 29 communions analyzed elsewhere in this report. The data for 29 communions is supplemented by the data of eight denominations included in an analysis of church membership and U.S. population by Roozen and Hadaway in David A. Roozen and Kirk C. Hadaway, eds., *Church and Denominational Growth* (Nashville: Abingdon Press, 1993), 393-395.

[18] These eleven denominations include nine of the communions in the composite 29 as well as The Episcopal Church and The United Methodist Church.

**Figure 12:** Trend in Membership as a Percent of U.S. Population, Eleven Mainline Protestant Denominations, Linear and Exponential Regression Based on Data for 1968-1985, with Actual Data 1986-1997

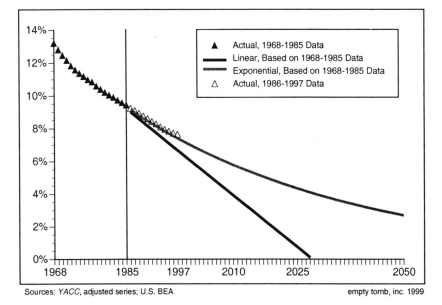

Sources: *YACC*, adjusted series; U.S. BEA                empty tomb, inc. 1999

**Figure 13:** Trend in Membership as a Percent of U.S. Population, Composite Denominations, Linear and Exponential Regression Based on Data for 1968-1985, with Actual Data 1986-1997

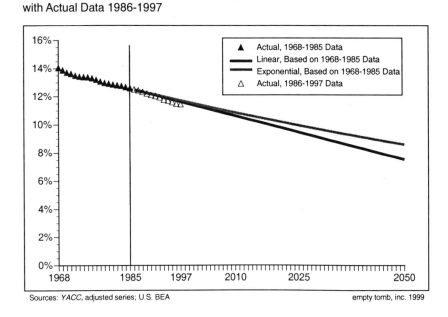

Sources: *YACC*, adjusted series; U.S. BEA                empty tomb, inc. 1999

levels in membership as a percent of U.S. population by the year 2050 for this set of communions. Figure 13 presents this information in graphic form.

***Membership in an Expanded Set of Communions.*** In addition to these composite denominations, membership data for the period 1968-1997 was available for seven additional Protestant communions, bringing the number of Protestant denominations with available data to 37. This expanded set of denominations includes some of the faster growing denominations in the U.S. When one considers whether the Protestant church in the U.S. is being marginalized as a social institution, a larger grouping of denominations provides a broader base from which to gain additional insight.

In 1968, these 37 Protestant denominations represented 42,747,548 members, and in 1997, a total of 43,918,877, an increase of 3%. Meanwhile, the overall population in the U.S. had been growing at a faster rate than the membership changes posted by these denominations. As a result, these communions were 21% of the U.S. population in 1968, and 16% in 1997.

Of course, the picture would be incomplete without the Roman Catholic Church, which included 47,468,333 members in 1968, and 61,563,769 members in 1997. Adding this membership data to

population in 1997, a smaller figure than that indicated by linear regression, suggesting the trend is closer to that predicted by linear regression than the exponential curve.

If the linear trend continues uninterrupted into the future, these composite denominations would represent 7.6% of the U.S. population in the year 2050. This number points to a decrease of 34% from 1997

that of the 37 Protestant communions considered above resulted in a total of 90,215,881 members in 1968. With the U.S. population at 200,745,000, these Christians constituted 45% of the 1968 U.S. population. By 1997, the group had grown to 105,482,646 members. However, with U.S. population having grown to 267,880,000, as of 1997, these Christians comprised 39% of the American population, a percent change of -12% from the 1968 base in the portion of the American population represented by these groups.

***The Response to the Trends.*** As in other sectors, trend lines in church giving and membership are designed to provide an additional source of information. Planning, evaluation and creative thinking are some of the types of constructive responses which can be made in light of projections. The information on church member giving and membership trends is offered as a possible planning tool.[19] The trend lines are not considered to be dictating what must happen, but rather as providing important indicators of what might happen if present conditions continue in an uninterrupted fashion. The results of the analysis may be useful as additional input to inform decisions by church leaders in the present.

The data reflects trends that raise important implications for the future. One might liken the projection to a symptom of illness. If a person is running a temperature of 104°, the choice would be to call the doctor or hope the fever runs its course. In either case, the body is communicating that there is a condition present which requires attention. Trends in church giving and membership, if used wisely, may be of assistance in addressing conditions present in the body of Christ in the U.S.

***Summary.*** The results of trend analysis do not dictate future behavior patterns, but rather indicate where present patterns are headed.

As of the 1997 data, it was not clear whether giving to Benevolences as a percentage of income paralleled a linear or exponential regression trend line. Giving to Congregational Finances followed an exponential curve more closely.

Church membership is declining as a percentage of U.S. population. The pattern is evident in a group of 11 mainline denominations, in the data set of composite denominations, and in an expanded group that includes 37 Protestant denominations and the Roman Catholic Church.

---

[19] For additional discussion of the implications of the trends, see Ronsvalle and Ronsvalle, *The State of Church Giving through 1991*, pp. 61-67.

chapter 6
# **HIGHLIGHTS**

*The Potential of the Church*

Is there a crisis in giving?

The people who discuss church giving the most tend to be church leaders and academics. These people also tend to be responsible for the organizational structure of the church. Church giving is very often associated with the ability of the congregation or the denomination to pay its bills. The insurance is paid? The pastor is paid? No programs were cut? "What a relief! There is no crisis."

Many members regard stewardship, or more specifically church giving, mainly as a means to pay the bills.[20]

However religion has the added component of spirituality. The purpose of the practice of religion is to relate to God. Given that the relationship between humans and their material goods, particularly money, is a repeated topic throughout the Bible, one may conclude from a religious point of view that there is more to money than paying the bills.

The classic giving standard is the tithe. Leaders debate whether, in the affluent culture that describes the late twentieth century U.S., the tithe is too low a standard. Others are concerned because it suggests legalism. However those who support the tithe note that it provides a biblically-based standard, against which church members can compare their

---

[20] John Ronsvalle and Sylvia Ronsvalle, *Behind the Stained Glass Windows: Money Dynamics in the Church* (Grand Rapids, MI: Baker Books, 1996), 121

own practice of their faith. Moreover, a churchwide average of ten percent giving would allow for a range in which some might give considerably more than ten percent, while some may not feel they can give, or refuse to consider giving, at that level.

The question at the beginning of this chapter can then be rephrased. If church members are richer than ever before, and yet are not approaching an average level of 10% giving, is there a crisis in giving?

In a world where 30,000 children die daily around the planet, many from preventable poverty conditions that would cost relatively little to correct, does it matter that Benevolences giving, including support for international missions, is shrinking?

In a culture where social health is declining—as evidenced by teenage suicide, violent crimes, highway deaths involving alcohol[21]—does it matter that the investment the church makes in society beyond itself through Benevolences is not growing?

***Potential Giving.*** The portion of income given to the church did not increase as incomes expanded between 1968 and 1997. Rather, giving declined as a portion of income, from 3.12% in 1968, to 2.56% in 1997.

How much money would have been available if giving had instead increased to an average of 10%?

At that level, church members would have donated an additional $121 billion dollars to their churches in 1997.

Further, suppose church members practiced their religion to such a degree that they were actually content. Suppose they were willing to say, "We have enough," and they directed the increased giving to the benefit of others.

Then, at the 10% average giving level, Benevolences would have increased from 0.41% to 8% of income.

If church members recognized the great need internationally, and continued the church tradition of reaching out globally, they could have focused 60% of the increase through their international denominational ministries.

The resulting $72 billion would allow the church to make a major impact on identified needs. For example, UNICEF has estimated that $2.5 billion more a year could stop most

---

[21] For a discussion of the social health in the United States, see Marc Miringoff and Marqu-Luisa Miringoff, *The Social Health of the Nation: How America Is Really Doing* (New York: Oxford University Press).

global under-five child deaths, and $7 billion additional each year would provide for universal primary education enrollment.

Another 20% of the increase could have been available for domestic ministry, totaling $24 billion.

Additional money would have been available for other activities, such as congregational missions education, including work trips to other countries, as well.

Figure 14 presents both the potential giving amounts, and two areas of global need that could be addressed.

Is there a crisis if church members are not fulfilling their potential for doing good to fellow human beings as a function of their faith? The answer to that question may appear different from a religious, rather than a bookkeeping, point of view.

**Figure 14:** Potential Additional Church Giving at a 1997 Average of 10%, and Illustrations of Global Need That Could Be Addressed_____

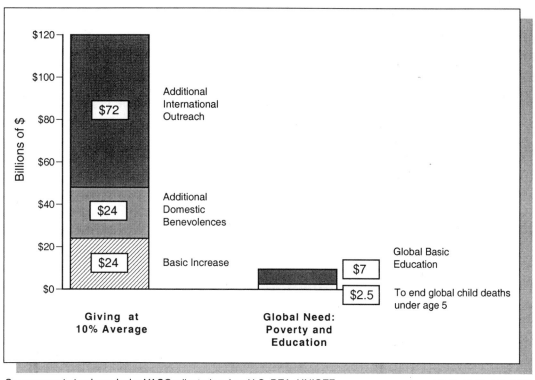

Source: empty tomb analysis; *YACC* adjusted series; U.S. BEA; UNICEF          empty tomb, inc. 1999

# NARRATIVE

The final section of chapter one in this volume reviews the amount of money that would have been donated, if the portion of income given in 1997 had been the same as it was in 1968.

The question may also be asked, what if giving had not only maintained the same level between 1968 and 1997 as a portion of income? Rather, what if church members had chosen to direct a larger portion of their increasing incomes to the church during this period? A classic standard for giving in the church has been a tithe, or 10% of income. Suppose congregation members had chosen to move to an average of 10% giving?

*Reaching the Tithe.* If giving had increased from 3.12% in 1968 to 10% in 1997, the level of income being donated to the church would have been 290% greater than the actual 1997 level of 2.56%.

In the chapter that compares alternative giving estimates, a revised series of total giving to religion is offered. This 1968-1997 series is keyed to the 1974 Filer Commission estimate of giving to religion. The 1968-1997 annual rate of change in the composite denominations was used to calculate figures for 1968-1973 and forward for 1975-1997, thus producing estimates of total giving to religion. In the Filer-based series, the 1997 estimate for total giving to religion was $49 billion.

If giving increased to an average of 10% giving, instead of $49 billion, $193 billion would have been donated to religion in 1997. An additional $144 billion would have been given to religion in the United States that year.

It was estimated that 84% of the U.S. population identifies with the historically Christian church—those communions and traditions, such as Roman Catholic, Orthodox, mainline Protestant, Pentecostal, evangelical, and Anabaptist, that profess a commitment to the historic tenets of the faith.

This figure of 84% can be applied to the additional $144 billion, to calculate the additional activity of the historically Christian Church, had giving been at the 10% level in 1997. These church members would have given $121 billion more at an average of 10% giving in 1997.[22]

One may continue this hypothetical discussion by supposing that these additional donations could have been directed not to the internal operations of the congregations, but rather to the broader mission of the church, as represented by Benevolences. Finally, one may suppose that denominations had adopted a proposed formula that 60% of this additional money be designated for international missions, and 20% be directed to domestic benevolences.[23]

The amount available for international ministries, had 60% of the $121 billion increase been directed to that category, would have been $72 billion. This amount is more than the $2.5 billion additional that has been estimated would stop most of the 11.6 million, global under-five child deaths each year, or the $7 billion additional each year that could provide primary education enrollment for all children.[24] The 20% of the $121 billion additional giving that would be available for domestic benevolences would have amounted to $24 billion.

After the 60% for international ministries, and 20% for domestic ministries, 20% of the increased giving is a basic increase. Part of this basic increase in Benevolences money could be used for mission

---

[22] An analysis based on information in George H. Gallup, Jr., R*eligion in America* (Princeton, NJ: The Princeton Religion Research Center, 1996), 42. This somewhat conservative estimate assumes that the religious giving was given by 100% of the U.S. population. If total religious giving comes only from the 91% of the U.S. population that claims a religious affiliation (see Gallup, p. 35), then the historically Christian component gave 92% of the total (84%/91%). In that case, rather than $121 billion, $132 billion of the total potential $144 billion additional would have been given by those who identify with the historically Christian church.

[23] UNICEF estimates that 32,000 children under the age of five die daily around the globe, mostly from preventable poverty conditions. UNICEF also estimates that 30,000 children under the age of five die annually in the United States (Carol Bellamy, *The State of the World's Children 1999* [New York: UNICEF, 1999], 97.) These statistics indicate that the great majority of need is in countries other than the U.S. The 60%/20% formula has been used in the authors' work with congregations. For a discussion of their international and domestic strategy approaches, see John Ronsvalle and Sylvia Ronsvalle, *The Poor Have Faces* (Grand Rapids, MI: Baker Books, 1992).

[24] James P. Grant, *The State of the World's Children 1990* (New York: Oxford University Press, 1990), 16, and Carol Bellamy, *The State of the World's Children 1999* (New York: UNICEF, 1999), 85.

education activities within the congregation, including work project trips internationally—as well as to cover additional direct expenses related to raising and distributing the additional funds.

If giving had increased to an average of 10%, and the additional funding had been directed to Benevolences, then giving would have increased from 0.41% of income to about 8%, with Congregational Finances staying at about the same levels. Figure 15 presents this information in graphic form.

***The Implications of the Hypothetical Scenarios.*** As the nonprofit sector receives more attention from society in general, the role it plays and can play is discussed and debated. One might review the above scenario in order to consider the question of whether the private sector, or more specifically the church, can take on additional responsibilities toward those who are in need in the U.S.

The data suggests that, if giving had increased from the actual 1997 level to an average giving level of 10%, there could have been an additional $24 billion available to assist people in need in the U.S. In theory, therefore, the church could have the resources necessary to impact domestic need, even while working at a significant level to alleviate global need in partnership with international sister churches.

However, it may also be noted that giving as a percentage of income did not increase at the rate that income did between 1968 and 1997, nor had it reached the 10% level by 1997. On the contrary, giving as a percentage of income declined by 18% between 1968 and 1997. More to the point, the portion of income going to Benevolences, the category that would take into account programs that address poverty conditions in the U.S. among other issues, declined by 38% in the 1968 to 1997 period. Further, the monetary potential of the church to address both domestic and global needs has remained culturally invisible in most church as well as secular media discussions.

The difference between potential and practice seems to be seated in the will, a category with broad religious implications.

**Figure 15:** Giving to Benevolences as a Portion of Income, at the 1997 Level, and at the Potential Level of 8%

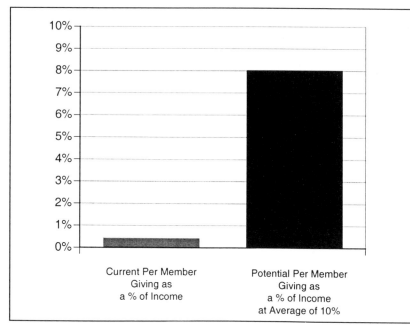

Sources: *YACC*, adjusted series; U.S. BEA                empty tomb, inc. 1999

## chapter 7

# HIGHLIGHTS

*Denominational Reports
and Other Estimates
of Charitable Giving*

Is there a "blame the victim" mentality operating in regard to the poor?

In the field of criminal justice, a major reorientation has taken place in the treatment and legal status of victims. Particularly in the areas of rape and domestic violence, a reevaluation of practices led to the conclusion that too often the victim was inappropriately blamed as a causal factor in the crime. Current legal policies have striven to redress this situation.

In the philanthropic arena, is there an unrecognized similar attitude in effect? The issue can be considered by presenting two alternative points of view.

If present giving patterns are healthy and reasonable, then if global and domestic need continues to exist, the conclusion is that the need is simply greater than can be met by charitable giving.

However, if present giving patterns have been declining in favor of, say, leisure spending, and therefore underfunding of programs to address need does not permit the development of solutions, but can only try to alleviate the worst of the suffering, then the discussion changes. If charitable contributions are at a relatively token level, or if levels have been declining instead of increasing, then those in need may be the victims of a human community that is out of kilter. At that point, the practice of philanthropy can be evaluated from within the larger context of the responsibility that accompanies increased resources. Not only religious values, but also civic duty, become reasonable ingredients in the discussion.

To make such a determination as to which of these two statements best describes the circumstances facing the poor, accurate charitable giving data is necessary.

It therefore becomes critically important that there is currently a void of such accurate charitable giving data.

The main source of information about giving in the U.S. is the American Association of Fund-Raising Counsel's *Giving USA* series. This annual survey is quoted widely in the media, as well as cited by government publications. However, the organization produces the information not as a scholarly resource, but rather as a public relations tool for use by its constituent members who are commercial, for-profit fund-raising businesses.

While AAFRC's purpose in publishing data may be understandable within its own context as a trade organization, the public and media make a mistake to use this information as a basis on which to form opinions about the practice of philanthropy. For example, the AAFRC data cannot be independently confirmed. Because of the way the organization has chosen to obtain its source data, AAFRC does not make its source data available for research purposes.

As a result, evaluation of the AAFRC numbers is limited to published, undocumented data. Nevertheless, some analyses can be conducted. For example, when a comparison between AAFRC's giving to religion series was compared to an estimate keyed to denominational data reports and a 1974 estimate from the Commission on Private Philanthropy and Public Needs, the AAFRC data was found to be significantly higher than the denominationally-based data.

Another source of philanthropic estimates comes from two publications, *The Chronicle of Philanthropy and The NonProfit Times*. Each publication has begun to present financial surveys of nonprofit organizations. In both cases, by measuring the organizations with the highest rate of growth from year to year, the publications do not provide information that is representative of the entire sector. Yet, other media use the information to judge the status of philanthropic activity as gauged by what has happened among the fastest growing organizations.

When presenting their information, *Giving USA* and the two philanthropy publication reports also do not take into account changes in population or after-tax income. Aggregate amounts may not indicate real growth in giving, if the per person donation, or the portion of income the donations represent, has been decreasing.

A comparison of AAFRC data in three formats found that aggregate data, whether in current or inflation-adjusted dollars, generally indicated an increase in donations. However, when population and after-tax income was taken into account, the same data indicated a decline in the level of donations on a per person basis as a portion of income over the period reported.

To obtain a more accurate understanding of philanthropy in the United States, certain steps could be taken. First, it would be useful if the annual Form 990, required by the Internal Revenue Service of many tax-exempt organizations, requested more specific information, for example, about whether the source of donations was from individuals, bequests, foundations, or corporations.

Second, the National Bureau of Economic Research could elevate the area of philanthropy to a standing program. Even as this group of scholars conducts economic research on topics such as the development of statistical measurements and the impact of public policies on economic performance, it could also provide an independent estimate of the level of charitable donations.

To date, the area of philanthropy has not received the quality attention it deserves. Important not only from an economic point of view, the voluntary practice of charitable giving is also a key element in a healthy democracy. Low expectations of charitable reporting have produced a climate in which little discriminating evaluation of the practice of philanthropy in the United States is possible.

A key step in helping people in need would be to obtain a realistic basis for determining the true level of charitable giving as practiced in the United States.

# NARRATIVE

*General Finding 1: A Review of AAFRC Giving USA Reports.* The American Association of Fund-Raising Counsel (AAFRC)'s *Giving USA* series serves as a useful tool for philanthropic development practitioners by providing a figure for the previous year's giving. Because of a void of other information on giving levels, the AAFRC data is by default used by the media, government, and the general public as the definitive source of national giving patterns. For example, AAFRC data serves as the source for philanthropic data in *The Statistical Abstract of the United States*.

While AAFRC's goal, as a trade organization, of serving its commercial, for-profit fund-raising constituency may be understandable, the use of AAFRC's data for other purposes compromises the call for a comprehensive, scholarly approach to assessing and reporting giving levels in the United States.

The tension inherent in this dual usage of AAFRC information is seen in an article that, among other things, deals with the fact that Giving USA distributes giving data for the most recent year as factual, while such data are actually projections:

> Some academic experts suggest that, due to the lag in the I.R.S. figures, the safest thing would be for *Giving USA* to stop issuing estimates for the previous year—and instead tell the public more precisely how much was given two years ago.

Ms. Kaplan says that approach is not appealing. "The longer you wait," she says, "the more accurate the data, but when you're fund raising and making public-policy decisions it's hard to wait."[25]

This focus on estimating individual giving for the most recent year has been a long-standing emphasis for *Giving USA* as seen in the following comments.

> Estimates of personal giving not only relate to the largest component of private philanthropy, they also are unavoidably based on data which are less complete and less timely than the data describing other groups of donors. This presents the AAFRC with a perennial problem because an important part of the value of *Giving USA* to its users is that it contains the most recent available estimates of private giving. This combination of frequency and reliability makes *Giving USA* unique among publications describing the private giving sector...
>
> *Giving USA* is published in the Spring of the year and from the time of its first issue in 1956 it has contained an estimate of private giving for the calendar year recently ended. This has imposed upon the AAFRC the task of making estimates under severe time constraints. For example, the estimate of personal giving for the year 1984 had to be made by mid-March 1985 so that it could appear in the 1985 edition of Giving USA which was released to the public in May 1985. In the estimation of personal giving this timetable of tight deadlines has presented the AAFRC with an especially difficult problem...[26]

The factors at work within the Association of Fund-Raising Counsel's *Giving USA* to develop a tool

helpful in public relations rather than an academically-sound record of philanthropy are systemic, and not due to the personnel involved at any given point in time. A chronic lack of scholarly rigor over the years of its publication is suggested by an evaluation from one of The Commission on Private Philanthropy and Public Needs (Filer Commission) research papers published by the United States Treasury Department in 1977:

> Our estimation method is described in Appendix D. In contrast to our systematic sampling procedure, the *Giving USA* total is based on a survey of major foundations. Their method of imputation for small foundations' grants is not specified in their published reports; however, it appears, from the language used, that the AAFRC uses some undescribed rules of thumb and intuition to make its estimates of total foundation activity from the surveys of a relatively small number of large foundations.[27]

**Comparison of estimates of giving to religion.** One area of AAFRC's methodology will be reviewed in this report. That is the category of giving to religion.

Religion is acknowledged as the single largest recipient category in the charitable arena. Estimates suggest almost 60% of every charitable dollar donated by individuals is designated for religion.[28] If donations to other organizations that have a religious affiliation but appear in another recipient category—such as the Salvation Army or Catholic Social Services that are defined as part of human services—were also considered, the portion of giving that is a function of religious activity would be higher.[29] Therefore, having an accurate estimate of giving to religion is important in determining the level of charitable financial activity in the United States.

---

[25] Harvey Lipman, "Report's Numbers Are No True Measure of Charity, Critics Say," *Chronicle of Philanthropy*, June 3, 1999, 30.

[26] Ralph L. Nelson, *The Amount of Total Personal Giving in the United States 1948-1982 with Projections to 1985 Using the Personal-Giving Estimating Model* (Alexandria, VA: United Way Institute, 1986), 1-2.

[27] Weisbrod, Burton A. and Stephen H. Long. "The Size of the Voluntary Nonprofit Sector: Concepts and Measures," *History, Trends, and Current Magnitudes*, Vol. 1 in the series, *Research papers Sponsored by The Commission on Private Philanthropy and Public Needs*. Department of the Treasury, Washington, DC, 1977, 360, n. 19

[28] AAFRC estimated that religion received 59% of individual charitable giving in 1997 ($72.69 billion of a total

individual giving level of $122.95 [Ann E. Kaplan, ed., *Giving USA 1999* (New York: American Association of Fund-Raising Counsel Trust for Philanthropy, 1999) 130, 132] ), while Independent Sector found that 57.5% of individual giving went to religious organizations for 1995 (Virginia A. Hodgkinson and Murray S. Weitzman, *Giving and Volunteering in the United States, 1996* (Washington, DC: Independent Sector, 1996), 25].

[29] For a discussion of the definition of religious charitable contributions, see Ronsvalle and Ronsvalle, "Denominational Giving Data and Other Sources of Religious Giving Information," *The State of Church Giving through 1991* (Champaign, IL: empty tomb, inc., 1993), 53-57.

The Filer Commission produced an estimate of giving to religion. That report estimated that in 1974, giving to religion was $11.7 billion.[30] This estimate was relatively close to the AAFRC estimate for 1974 of $11.84 billion.[31]

When revising its historical series, AAFRC did not choose to key its religion data to the Filer Commission estimate of giving to religion.

AAFRC did revise its religion estimates for 1987 through 1997 based on the percent change in receipts for denominations that publish data in the *Yearbook of American and Canadian Churches* series.[32]

In theory, one could follow a methodology for religion similar to that AAFRC used for the categories of education and health, in this case keying 1974 to the Filer Commission estimate, and then calculate estimates for the years 1968 to 1973, and 1975 to 1997, based on an external source of data. The external source of data could be the same that AAFRC used to revise its 1987 through 1996 data, a set of denominations that publish data in the *Yearbook of American and Canadian Churches* series. This revised approach would remedy the estimates for those years when AAFRC did not calculate a figure for religion, but rather considered it a "residual" category, having the recipient category of religion absorb the difference between AAFRC's estimate of total giving and the sum of its estimates for other recipient categories.

The starting base in this approach could be the Filer Commission estimate of $11.7 billion for 1974. The amount of change from year to year, calculated for 1968 to 1973 and also 1975 to 1997, could be the annual percentage change in the 29 denominations analyzed in other chapters of this report. This calculation yields a total of $8 billion given to religion in 1968, and $49 billion in 1997. These figures contrast with the AAFRC estimate of $8.42 billion in 1968 and $72.69 billion in 1997. Table 16 presents this data.

Comparing these two estimate series, one may observe that the two series are within a few percentage

points of each other for two years on either side of 1974, the year of the Filer estimate to which the denominational-based series is keyed. The estimates vary from 11% to 13% through 1981. AAFRC methodology does not indicate when religion became a residual recipient category, although the differences in the data series suggests some change in AAFRC methodology took place between 1976 and 1977.

In 1982, while the denominational-based estimate series continues to change at a consistent rate, the AAFRC estimate series begins to expand more rapidly from year to year. The percentage difference grew from 17% in 1982 to 47% in 1997.

Although AAFRC revised its data for 1987 through 1997 based on a different methodology than the residual definition, those latter estimates continued to build on the earlier years' data, during which religion was a residual category absorbing any difference between AAFRC's individual giving estimate and its sum of the other recipient category estimates.

In previous editions of *The State of Church Giving* series, more detailed discussion has been devoted to AAFRC's methodology in developing its Total and Individual giving estimates. At this point, it may be of interest to note the results from substituting the alternative giving to religion series for the AAFRC series to develop alternative Total and Individual giving figures.

The published AAFRC 1997 Total contributions figure in *Giving USA 1999* was $158 billion. When the revised Filer-based religion figure is substituted for the 1997 AAFRC religion estimate, that Total figure is revised to $134 billion.

In individual giving, instead of $123 billion given in 1997 as AAFRC projected, the figure would be $99.71 billion, substituting the Filer-based religion figure for the AAFRC estimate of giving to religion.

**Inability to verify data.** Difficulty in verifying the AAFRC *Giving USA* data can be seen from a more

---

[30] *Research Papers Sponsored by The Commission on Private Philanthropy and Public Needs, Vol. 1, History, Trends, and Current Magnitudes*, Department of the Treasury, Washington, DC, 1977, 136.

[31] Kaplan, *Giving USA 1999*, 132.

[32] Kaplan, *Giving USA 1999*, 151. AAFRC suggests that its 1986 data matches that of other religion sources. The 1986 estimate is close to the estimate in the first edition of the Independent Sector report, *From Belief to Commitment*

by Virginia A. Hodgkinson, Murray Weitzman, and Arthur D. Kirsch, eds. (Washington, DC: Independent Sector, 1988). However, the next Independent Sector figure in Virginia A. Hodgkinson, Murray Weitzman, et al., *From Belief to Commitment* (Washington, DC: Independent Sector, 1992) varied from the AAFRC estimate. For a discussion of the latter data, see Ronsvalle and Ronsvalle, *The State of Church Giving through 1991*, 41-42.

**Table 16:** Giving to Religion, AAFRC Series and Denomination-Based Series, 1968-1997, Aggregate, Billions of Dollars and Percent Difference

| Year | AAFRC Series[33] (Billions $) | Denomination-Based Series Keyed to 1974 Filer Series (Billions $) | Percent Difference between AAFRC and Denomination-Based Series |
|------|------|------|------|
| 1968 | $8.42 | $8.01 | 5% |
| 1969 | $9.02 | $8.33 | 8% |
| 1970 | $9.34 | $8.66 | 8% |
| 1971 | $10.07 | $9.14 | 10% |
| 1972 | $10.10 | $9.79 | 3% |
| 1973 | $10.53 | $10.70 | -2% |
| 1974 | $11.84 | $11.70 | 1% |
| 1975 | $12.81 | $12.75 | 0% |
| 1976 | $14.18 | $13.87 | 2% |
| 1977 | $16.98 | $15.02 | 13% |
| 1978 | $18.35 | $16.41 | 12% |
| 1979 | $20.17 | $18.15 | 11% |
| 1980 | $22.23 | $20.07 | 11% |
| 1981 | $25.05 | $22.14 | 13% |
| 1982 | $28.06 | $23.99 | 17% |
| 1983 | $31.84 | $25.60 | 24% |
| 1984 | $35.55 | $27.70 | 28% |
| 1985 | $38.21 | $29.45 | 30% |
| 1986 | $41.68 | $31.09 | 34% |
| 1987 | $43.51 | $32.40 | 34% |
| 1988 | $45.15 | $33.66 | 34% |
| 1989 | $47.77 | $35.45 | 35% |
| 1990 | $49.79 | $36.97 | 35% |
| 1991 | $50.00 | $38.36 | 30% |
| 1992 | $54.91 | $39.43 | 39% |
| 1993 | $56.29 | $40.50 | 39% |
| 1994 | $60.21 | $43.36 | 39% |
| 1995 | $66.26 | $44.20 | 50% |
| 1996 | $70.66 | $47.72 | 48% |
| 1997 | $72.69 | $49.45 | 47% |

contemporary setting than the 1977 Filer Commission report. In inflation-adjusted 1998 dollars, *Giving USA 1999* reported that Human Services decreased from $14.97 billion in 1989 to $12.86 billion in 1997, and then jumped 25.1% to $16.08 in 1998.

This increase was of interest from a research point of view. Previously, an analysis had been conducted due to suggestions from various quarters that religious giving might have been going down because donors were instead increasing their giving to the types of organizations represented in the Human Services category. A comparison of data published by AAFRC had found this hypothesis to be false through 1997

(see "Per capita giving to other recipient categories, 1968-1997" below). Instead, the analysis indicated that donations to Human Services had decreased more than had donations to Religion.

Therefore, it seemed important to obtain the most recent AAFRC data in order to replicate the calculations for the latest AAFRC estimate for giving to Human Services organizations. The goal was to explore the possible reasons for the 1997 to 1998 increase. This increase might be due to: (1) an increase in giving to Human services; (2) a change in accounting procedures on the part of the reporting organizations; (3) a change in the sample of

[33] Kaplan, *Giving USA 1999*, 132.

organizations, introducing a new factor in the calculation; or (4) some other factor. Regarding the point about the sampling process, in the Methodology section, under a subsection entitled, "Giving to Other Recipient Categories," *Giving USA 1999* states:

> The AAFRC Trust for Philanthropy tripled its sample size and drew a new sample for the 1998 estimate. For recipient categories, including health and education, which are discussed in more detail above, the percentage change in giving from 1997 to 1998 was used to calculate the change in giving to each recipient category.[34]

In order to rule out the possibility that the increase in giving to Human services was an artifact due to a change in sampling methods, a request was sent to AAFRC for the source data for data years 1996, 1997 and 1998, to be used for research purposes. The request included:

> The list of Human Services organizations whose giving data was used to estimate giving to organizations in Human Services for each of the three years.
>
> The actual giving data for each of these Human Service organizations for each of the three years.
>
> The methodology used to extrapolate the final giving to Human Service organizations for each of the three years.

In response, an AAFRC representative indicated that the information was not available due to a "promise of confidentiality" made in AAFRC's survey instrument, a short questionnaire which asks for, among other things, publicly available "charitable revenue" information. It was further explained that "If we did not make this promise, we would publish a list of respondents with the information as I believe this would make our publication more valuable...Unfortunately, the response rate is much better when this arrangement is pursued." A sample copy of the survey instrument was enclosed.

Samples of the one-page Survey Form for *Giving USA 1998* and the less detailed one-page Survey Form for *Giving USA 1999* both include the sentence, "Financial information from this questionnaire will remain completely confidential." Each form asks for three dollar amounts: Total Revenue, Charitable Revenue Only, and Bequests. Immediately below the space for Charitable Revenue Only, the 1999 Survey

Form states, "Charitable revenue figures can be pulled directly from *Line 1a of IRS Form 990*." Thus, for at least one major category in its calculation, the information that AAFRC promises to keep confidential is otherwise publicly available.

If the information used to develop the AAFRC estimates of giving cannot be reviewed and confirmed by other researchers, this information is not useful as a sound estimate of philanthropic activity in the United States.

***General Finding 2: Limits to Self-Report Information.*** Survey instruments, which have been proven useful in yes/no or multiple choice format questions dealing with voting patterns or general public opinion, have not, at least as used by commercial survey houses, proven to be uniformly valid for use in assessing individual giving patterns over the biannual periods covered by Independent Sector's *Giving and Volunteering in the United States* series. Previous editions in *The State of Church Giving* series have considered the wide variation that exists between one year's data and the next when surveys are used to estimate giving behavior.[35]

***General Finding 3: "Giving" Not Defined.*** More careful discrimination in reporting would assist the public in distinguishing between the different meanings of "giving" as included in media coverage. Namely, the general public may assume that a report on giving refers to contributions given by individuals, when, in fact, it may refer to composite donations by individuals, bequests, foundations and corporations.

***General Finding 4: Adjusting for Population and Income.*** Adjustment for population and after-tax income in giving analyses by recipient category, and the reporting of individual donation levels, would assist the public in accurately comprehending its collective behavior. Since individual giving is estimated to constitute over three-quarters of all giving, a first-approximation evaluation of aggregate giving that takes into account both population and after-tax income, would provide useful information. In the near future, Form 990-based estimates of individual giving within each recipient sector would also be of great use.

**Aggregate compared with per capita data.** AAFRC data is generally considered in aggregate numbers. These totals indicate how much various charitable categories, such as Human Services or Education, had received. The focus of the present

---

[34] Kaplan, *Giving USA 1999*, 152.

[35] For example, see John Ronsvalle and Sylvia Ronsvalle, *The State of Church Giving through 1995* (Champaign, IL: empty tomb, inc., 1997), 65-81.

report is on trends in individual giving. For this reason, a review of the AAFRC data converted to a per capita basis may be useful.

Per capita data takes into account not only the changes in the amounts given, but also changes in the population of donors.

When the AAFRC data—the series as published rather than the revised denomination-based series discussed above—takes population into account, the positive trend noted from year to year is affected.

In current dollars, according to the AAFRC aggregate individual data, giving increased from $14.75 billion in 1968 to $122.95 billion in 1997. When those aggregate numbers are divided by the population, the figures also show an increase on a per capita basis. In 1968, according to this data, per capita giving was $73.48 and in 1997, it was $458.97.

Similarly, current dollar per member giving increased in the composite denominations, as shown in Table 1 of this report's chapter one, from $96.69 in 1968 to $554.30 in 1997.

**Giving as a percent of income.** One telling indicator in an evaluation of philanthropy is how much a contribution represents of the individual's overall income. In this way, one might attribute a weight to the value that people place on charitable activity in the context of their total spending patterns.

In 1968, U.S. per capita disposable personal income in current dollars was $3,101, and in 1997 it was $21,633. Disposable personal income is the category of choice because it takes into account the change in personal

taxes during the 1968-1996 period. Although AAFRC does consider individual giving as a portion of income, it uses personal income which does not reflect changes in the level of taxes paid by individuals donating to charity.[36]

**Per capita individual giving as a percent of income.** When the per capita AAFRC estimate of individual giving is taken as a portion of disposable personal income, it becomes apparent that in 1968, charitable giving represented 2.37% of Americans' average income, while in 1997 it represented 2.12%, a decline of 10% in the portion of U.S. per capita disposable personal income contributed to charity.

**Per capita giving to religion.** The aggregate data in Table 16 was divided by U.S. population to produce a per capita figure for both the AAFRC giving to religion series and the denomination-based series. The two series were then converted to giving as a percentage of U.S. disposable personal income. The comparison is presented in Figure 16 below.

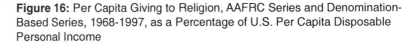

**Figure 16:** Per Capita Giving to Religion, AAFRC Series and Denomination-Based Series, 1968-1997, as a Percentage of U.S. Per Capita Disposable Personal Income

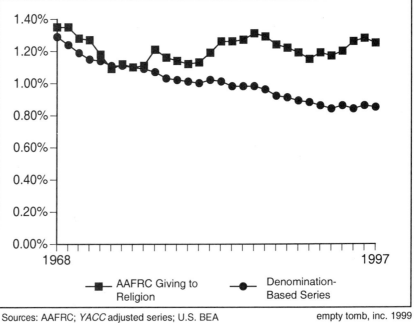

Sources: AAFRC; *YACC* adjusted series; U.S. BEA

empty tomb, inc. 1999

[36] Ann E. Kaplan, ed., *Giving USA 1998,* (New York: American Association of Fund-Raising Counsel Trust for Philanthropy, 1998), 34.

**Per capita giving to other recipient categories, 1968-1997.** Considering giving to various recipient categories on a per capita basis as well may provide a different picture than indicated by the aggregate data. A comparison is presented in Table 17 below.

It should be noted that the recipient categories presented by AAFRC do not make a distinction by source of contribution. AAFRC does state that the majority of donations to religion comes from individuals. However, AAFRC does not provide figures within each of the various recipient categories as to the amount of donations from each source, the four being: individuals, bequests, foundations, and corporations. Therefore, the comparison below is only approximate. It does, however, suggest important factors to be taken into consideration when discussing trends in charitable giving.

Table 17 presents the AAFRC published data for the recipient categories of: religion; education; health;

human services; arts, culture, and humanities; and public/society benefit.[37] Since data for the recipient categories of environment/wildlife and international affairs is provided only for years beginning with 1987, these categories are not included. The category of giving to foundations has current dollar data only back to 1978, and likewise is not considered in this table. The category of unallocated is also not included.

From this table, it is apparent once again that giving to religion receives the highest level of charitable giving support. Aggregate giving in both current and inflation-adjusted dollars increased. However, as a portion of U.S. per capita disposable personal income, the amount of giving to religion decreased by 7%. Table 17 uses the AAFRC estimate of giving to religion series. When the denomination-based series data was used instead, the portion of U.S. disposable personal income donated to religion declined from 1.29% in 1968 to 0.85% in 1997, a decline of 34%.

**Table 17:** AAFRC Giving to Recipient Categories, 1968 and 1997, Aggregate, Current and Inflation-Adjusted 1998 Dollars (Billions of Dollars), and Per Capita as a Percent of U.S. Disposable Personal Income, with Percent Change 1968-1997

|  | Religion | | | Education | | |
|---|---|---|---|---|---|---|
|  | Aggregate (Billions $) | | Per Capita | Aggregate (Billions $) | | Per Capita |
|  | Current $ | Infl.-Adj.'98 $ | % Income | Current $ | Infl.-Adj.'98 $ | % Income |
| 1968 | $8.42 | $39.44 | 1.35% | $2.38 | $11.15 | 0.38% |
| 1997 | $72.69 | $73.83 | 1.25% | $22.16 | $22.51 | 0.38% |
| % Change | 763% | 87% | -7% | 831% | 102% | 0% |

|  | Health | | | Human Services | | |
|---|---|---|---|---|---|---|
|  | Aggregate (Billions $) | | Per Capita | Aggregate (Billions $) | | Per Capita |
|  | Current $ | Infl.-Adj.'98 $ | % Income | Current $ | Infl.-Adj.'98 $ | % Income |
| 1968 | $2.08 | $9.74 | 0.33% | $2.31 | $10.82 | 0.37% |
| 1997 | $14.03 | $14.25 | 0.24% | $12.66 | $12.86 | 0.22% |
| % Change | 575% | 46% | -28% | 448% | 19% | -41% |

|  | Arts, Culture, and Humanities | | | Public/Society Benefit | | |
|---|---|---|---|---|---|---|
|  | Aggregate (Billions $) | | Per Capita | Aggregate (Billions $) | | Per Capita |
|  | Current $ | Infl.-Adj.'98 $ | % Income | Current $ | Infl.-Adj.'98 $ | % Income |
| 1968 | $0.60 | $2.83 | 0.10% | $0.43 | $2.00 | 0.07% |
| 1997 | $10.62 | $10.79 | 0.18% | $8.38 | $8.52 | 0.14% |
| % Change | 1670% | 281% | 90% | 1849% | 326% | 109% |

[37] Kaplan, *Giving USA 1999*, 132-135.

All the categories in Table 17 showed an increase in terms of aggregate giving in both current and inflation-adjusted dollars. However, giving as a percentage of income provides additional information. Per capita giving as a portion of income to education remained the same during this period. However, giving to health decreased 28%, and giving to human services declined 41%.

The two recipient categories that show an increase are arts, culture and humanities, and the category of public/society benefit. While neither group represented more than 0.2% of per capita giving as a portion of income in 1997, both posted increases of 90% and 109% respectively, between 1968 and 1997, in contrast to the other categories in the table.

Figure 17 (see page 64) presents two views of five recipient categories: education; health; human services; arts, culture, and humanities; and public/society benefit. The view in the left column presents the aggregate AAFRC data in both current and inflation-adjusted 1997 dollars. This is the view presented in the *Giving USA* series for each recipient category. The view in the right column for each recipient category presents the AAFRC data on a per capita basis as a percentage of U.S. per capita disposable personal income.

The decline to human services as a portion of per capita disposable personal income is an important indicator. Often, when the trends in religious giving discussed in other chapters of this report have been presented, a frequently proposed hypothesis has been that individuals have withdrawn giving from their churches and directed it to other helping agencies. Since giving to religion declined by 7% using the AAFRC published series, or by 34% using the revised denomination-based series—while per capita giving to human services declined by 41% as a portion of income—the data does not support the conventional wisdom that giving to religion has decreased because there was a withdrawal from religious giving in favor of specialized human service agencies.

***General Finding 5: Other Measurements of Nonprofit Activity.*** Major philanthropic media, namely, *The Chronicle of Philanthropy* and *The NonProfit Times*, in recent years have issued annual reports on giving, "The Philanthropy 400" and the "NPT 100," respectively. Neither group adjusts its reports of aggregate dollar increases for either population or after-tax income. In addition, these reports have introduced a new source of statistical error, namely that stemming from statistical regression, also referred to as regression toward the mean.

Examples of approaches taken by other economic sectors are useful.

- To measure changes in the stock market, the Dow Jones compares a fixed set of 30 industrial stocks in a standard portfolio that is periodically adjusted. In contrast, were the Dow Jones to use an approach similar to that incorporated in the nonprofit organization lists, the measurement would be made by taking the top 30 stocks in any given period and measuring how those stocks changed from the previous period. In that case, the stock market reports would always reflect the most artificially ebullient outcome.

- To measure inflation, the prices of a "market basket" of items is compared from one period to the next. To measure a changing mix of items based on those that increased the most in price from one period to the next would not provide a valid measurement of inflation.

- To track population growth in the United States, one would compare the numbers for all the counties in the country. To measure the populations of the 100 counties that grew the most from last year to the current year would not provide a valid measurement of overall population changes in the U.S.

The nonprofit organization surveys by the professional philanthropic publications have a wider effect than informing only a professional constituency. For example, a nationally-syndicated headline of a 1999 AP story with a Washington byline read, "Donations to Charities Jump 16 percent in 1998." The first sentence of the story continued, "Donors gave 16 percent more in contributions to the nation's most popular charities last year than in 1997, a survey of the top 400 charities shows."[38]

---

[38] Quoted from the AP, Washington byline, in *The Champaign-Urbana News Gazette*, November 1, 1999, A2.

It therefore behooves these philanthropy publications to provide a valid picture of the state of philanthropy. Developing a stable "market basket" or "portfolio" of representative nonprofit organizations to measure over time would avoid the statistical error resulting from the changing composition of the highest performing organizations in the present surveys.

A useful, basic discussion, designed for journalists, of the importance of considering changes in population, as well as an introduction to statistical regression, is found in *The New Precision Journalism,* first published in 1973 (Bloomington and Indianapolis: Indiana University Press, 1991). As noted on the book jacket, the author, Philip Meyer, is William Rand Kenan, Jr., Professor of Journalism at the University of North Carolina at Chapel Hill.

***General Finding 6: Religion Underrepresented.*** *The Chronicle of Philanthropy*'s Philanthropy 400 and *The NonProfit Time*'s NPT 100 treat religion in a way that contributes to a narrowly secularized view of the United States. For example, in the *Chronicle*'s "Causes That Garnered the Most Support Section," Education is listed at $11.6 billion while Religion is $1.6 billion plus a separate listing for Jewish federations at $0.8 billion.[39]

The Philanthropy 400 writes, "For the most part, the Philanthropy 400 does not include churches, which are not required to make their finances public. A few agreed to fill out the survey form and are included in the list."[40]

A curious list of 27 "Religious Groups" includes one congregation, two denominations, which together are comprised of 8,025 congregations, two denominational foundations, one council of churches, a few denominational agencies, and a number of parachurch organizations. In a separate listing of "Jewish Federations," 15 organizations are listed.

Under Religious Groups, one of the denominations, The United Church of Christ (Cleveland) which is asterisked, indicating that it "Includes affiliates," lists a "Private support" amount of $26,307,308. The second denomination, Christian and Missionary Alliance (Colorado Springs) which is also asterisked, indicating that it "Includes affiliates," lists a "Private support" amount of $45,027,009.[41] In contrast to these numbers, The United Church of Christ reported in the 1999 *Yearbook of American and Canadian Churches* a 1997 Total Contributions amount of $721,356,966,[42] while the Christian and Missionary Alliance in the same edition of the *Yearbook* reported a 1997 figure of $249,484,961.[43]

There is a reasonable basis for the Philanthropy 400 to make use of data reported to the *Yearbook of American and Canadian Churches* to obtain giving figures for religious denominations.

Consider that, for a number of organizations, the 1999 Philanthropy 400 reports only the Income category of "Private support," with no information listed for the breakdown between "Program services" and "Fund raising." For example, this is true for 37th ranked University of Michigan (Ann Arbor), 40th ranked University of Washington (Seattle), and 51st ranked Indiana University System (Bloomington).[44]

In addition:

> Contribution figures for most colleges and universities come from an annual survey conducted by the Council for Aid to Education, a New York organization that monitors charitable giving.

> Those data are used because public colleges and universities are not required to fill out a Form 990 and, as a result, getting an accurate comparison of public and private institutions can be difficult.[45]

Thus, a comparable situation exists for denominations' annually aggregated "Total Contributions" congregational data reported in the *Yearbook of American and Canadian Churches.* The *Yearbook* reported financial data for around 40 denominations for a recent two-year period, with mostly 1997 financial data in the 1999 edition of the *Yearbook* totaling somewhat over $20 billion.

---

[39] "Causes That Garnered the Most Support," *Chronicle of Philanthropy*, November 4, 1999, 51.

[40] "How the Philanthropy 400 Rankings on Contributions Were Compiled," *Chronicle of Philanthropy*, November 4, 1999, 42.

[41] Rankings by Type of Organization," *Chronicle of Philanthropy*, November 4, 1999, 44-45.

[42] *Yearbook of American and Canadian Churches*

(Nashville: Abingdon, 1999), 358.

[43] *Yearbook of American and Canadian Churches,* 1999, 356.

[44] "The Philanthropy 400," *Chronicle of Philanthropy*, November 4, 1999, 33.

[45] "How the Philanthropy 400 Rankings on Contributions Were Compiled," *Chronicle of Philanthropy*, November 4, 1999, 42.

**Figure 17:** AAFRC Recipient Category Data, 1968-1997

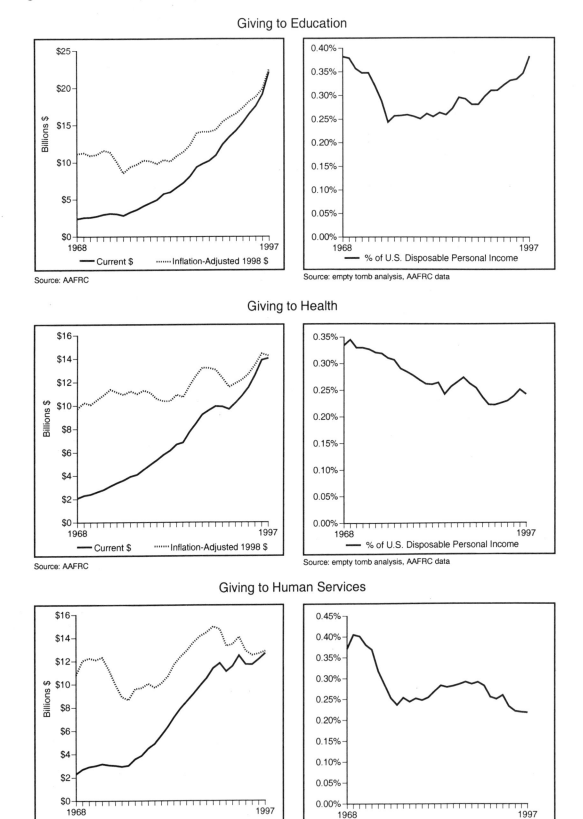

**Figure 17:** AAFRC Recipient Category Data, 1968-1997, Continued

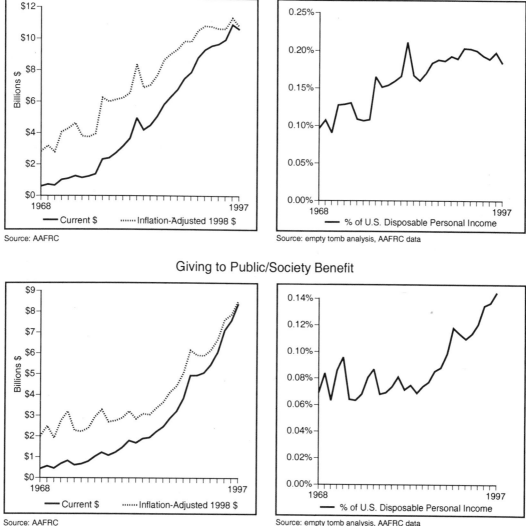

With national discussion focusing increasingly on the positive role of religion, it would be helpful for the public to have a clearer picture of the role that religion plays in the list of philanthropic organizations.

***Developing a Valid Measure of Philanthropic Activity.*** Whether inadvertently or not, the net effect of the results presented in *Giving USA*, *The Chronicle of Philanthropy* and *The NonProfit Times*, and the reporting of these results widely in other media—results which are not corrected for population or after-tax income and/or which report a distorted view by regarding the top performers in the field as representative—is to provide an overly high estimate of the growth in giving. The source of estimates of giving may well need to come from an entity that could

not be influenced by a professionally interested constituency through advertising or organizational membership.

An accurate picture of the practice of philanthropy would require an approach different from those presently being pursued. Three major ways to estimate individual giving exist, although the third listed below may have the most to recommend it.

The first approach is survey data based on self-report. This approach, used extensively by Independent Sector's *Giving and Volunteering in the United States* series, yields estimates of overall individual giving, as well as estimates by use, and estimates for itemizers and nonitemizers.

65

A weakness in this approach is that, at a number of important points, this self-report data, as gathered to date, has not proven reliable in estimating giving trends when comparing one year to another.

A second data source is the aggregated data on charitable deductions claimed by itemizers that the U.S. Treasury Department publishes.

There are three problems with this approach for estimating individual giving. First, no reliable estimate of giving by nonitemizers is available. Second, no systematic, annually updated method for correction for overreporting, commonly referred to as tax evasion or tax cheating, is applied to this data as reported in the I.R.S. *Statistics of Income Bulletin.* A 1989 study found overreporting of 7.2% in 1982.[46] There are indications that tax cheating in other areas has increased since that time.[47] Third, no correction for in-kind deductions, such as donations of used clothing, furniture and household items, etc., is made for this data.

The third source is Form 990 reports collected by the IRS. Form 990 data reports on how much organizations receive, and is therefore perhaps one of the better potential sources of estimates of giving available.

One major problem with this data is that Form 990 does not, as of the present, request contributions data broken down by the major categories of Individuals, Bequests, Foundations and Corporations. This should not be a major problem for charities to provide since, the more likely it is that charities receive contributions from sources other than individuals, the more likely it is that gifts from these sources are tracked by category for internal management purposes.

A second potential problem with Form 990 data that is mentioned in philanthropic circles from time to time is its accuracy. One mitigating factor, however is that the larger the amounts involved and the greater the potential source of error, the more likely that the organization's data is audited and accurately reported.

A third factor leading to a lack of comprehensiveness of Form 990 data is that certain organizations are not required to file a Form 990, including some religious organizations. The following groups are not required to file:

1. A church, an interchurch organization of local units of a church, a convention or association of churches, an integrated auxiliary of a church (such as a men's or women's organization, religious school, mission society, or youth group).

2. Church-affiliated organizations that are exclusively engaged in managing funds or maintaining retirement programs...

3. A school below college level affiliated with a church or operated by a religious order.

4. A mission society sponsored by, or affiliated with, one or more churches or church denominations, if more than half of the society's activities are conducted in, or directed at, persons in foreign countries.

5. An exclusively religious activity of any religious order.

11. A religious or apostolic organization described in section 501(d). Use Form 1065, U.S. Partnership Return of Income.[48]

However, a systematic review of giving data from the *Yearbook of American and Canadian Churches,* along with a "Religious/Secular" categorization of all organizations required to file Form 990s, would go far toward providing a firm base for estimating religious giving in the United States.

A common misunderstanding is that "Religious" organizations, in general, do not need to file Form 990s. For example, one published report stated that "Religious organizations, federally chartered groups such as the American Red Cross, and charities with annual revenues of less than $25,000 are not required to file a return."[49]

---

[46] Joel Slemrod, "Are Estimated Tax Elasticities Really Just Evasion Elasticities? The Case of Charitable Contributions," *The Review of Economics and Statistics*, Vol. LXXI, No. 3, August, 1989, 522. The application of the results of this paper to estimates of individual giving is discussed in Ralph L. Nelson, "A Revised Methodology for Estimating Total Personal Giving in the United States, with Preliminary Estimates for the Period 1984-1992," *Voluntas* 4.3 (1993), 245.

[47] Frank Lalli, Managing Editor in "Editor's Notes," quotes Lester Thurow, dean of MIT's Sloan School of Management

as stating, "Cheating is on the rise...We have a lot more of it today than 20 years ago," in *Money*, April, 1991, 5. In the same issue, Marguerite T. Smith, in "Who Cheats on Their Income Taxes," quotes Thurow, "The growing tax gap tells me that the public thinks it's more acceptable to cheat," p. 103.

[48] Internal Revenue Service, "1998 Instructions for Form 990 and Form 990-EZ," (Washington, D.C.), 2.

[49] "Technology: Charity Data Goes On Line—and Then Off," *Chronicle of Philanthropy*, November 4, 1999, 69.

Yet, a number of Religious organizations, such as the Billy Graham Evangelistic Association—some of which often are, perhaps questionably, referred to as "parachurch" organizations—file Form 990s, including the Salvation Army, World Vision, and Habitat for Humanity International, each of which is in the top 25 of The Philanthropy 400.[50] Three of the top four organizations in the NPT 100's six-organization Relief/Development category [51] are Religious; two of these three Religious organizations file Form 990.[52]

Of these three alternative sources for charitable giving data, an enhanced Form 900—which requests information categorized according to the four source contributions of Individuals, Bequests, Foundations, and Corporations—shows the greatest promise of providing a reliable and valid source of data.

This Form 990 data would need to be supplemented by congregational and denominational contributions data. The current, annual data in the *Yearbook of American and Canadian Churches* provides a base from which to estimate this area.

In addition, special effort needs to be taken to determine how many funds, having passed through a third nonprofit, fund-raising party, such as the United Ways, were directed to religious organizations. For example, of the $1.0 billion listed in The Philanthropy 400 for "United Ways,"[53] how much of that amount was received by organizations included in the "Human services and youth" category that would also define themselves as Religious?

*Systemic Recommendations.* There are two general areas which could improve philanthropic reporting.

**Proposed Form 990 changes.** Three improvements in regard to the Form 990 distributed and collected by The U.S. Treasury Department would assist in an understanding of philanthropic data.

1. Form 990 could request figures for private contributions by source, exclusive of in-kind contributions, from the following four categories:

a. Individuals

b. Bequests

c. Foundations

d. Corporations

2. Form 990 could request information as to whether an organization is Religious or Secular, and then, in addition, the amounts any given organization spends on specific broad categories of activity, as employed in *Giving USA*. These categories include Religion (for Religious organizations, this would refer to religion-specific expenditures, in contrast to religiously motivated expenditures for activities in other categories such as those that follow in this list); Education; Health; Human Services; Arts, Culture, Humanities; Public/Society Benefit; Environment/ Wildlife; International Affairs; plus an omnibus "Other" category.

3. The Treasury Department could electronically enter (if the information is not already submitted in that form) and publish, key income and expense statistics from Form 990s in individual and summary format.

This last point is not a new idea. It is interesting to note that over 20 years ago, in the landmark 1977 Department of the Treasury "Filer Commission" publication, the academically-based authors of a commissioned paper optimistically wrote, "The IRS is in the process of computerizing the Form 990 returns. It may be possible before long to obtain data for all filers, making it unnecessary to estimate totals from a sample, as we have done."[54]

A positive development in this regard is that Philanthropic Research and the National Center for Charitable Statistics at the Urban Institute have been working with the I.R.S. to list Form 990 information on a Web site «www.guidestar.org». *The Chronicle of Philanthropy* reported that "Eventually, the organization plans to post Forms 990 for all of the approximately 220,000 charities that it estimates are required to file the document."[55] One would hope

---

[50] "The Philanthropy 400," *Chronicle of Philanthropy*, November 4, 1999, p. 33.

[51] "Relief/Development," *NonProfit Times*, November 1999, 42.

[52] Philanthropic Research, Inc.; "Billy Graham Evangelistic Association"; "Salvation Army World Service Office (SAWSO)"; "Habitat for Humanity International"; "World Vision, Inc."; 1999 (accessed: 11/19/99); <www.guidestar.org>.

[53] "Causes That Garnered the Most Support," *The Chronicle of Philanthropy*, November 4, 1999, p. 51.

[54] Weisbrod, Burton A. and Stephen H. Long. "The Size of the Voluntary Nonprofit Sector: Concepts and Measures," *History, Trends, and Current Magnitudes*, Vol. 1 in the series, *Research papers Sponsored by The Commission on Private Philanthropy and Public Needs*. Department of the Treasury, Washington, DC, 1977, 360, n. 17.

[55] "Technology: Charity Data Goes On Line—and Then Off," *Chronicle of Philanthropy*, November 4, 1999, 69.

that the Department of the Treasury remains strongly supportive—financially, if need be—of this effort to post all of the Form 990s, if the Treasury Department, itself, does not take on the responsibility of providing this information to the public.

**Establishing a nonprofit program in the NBER.** Obtaining a valid measurement of philanthropic activity in the United States could be furthered by establishing a NonProfit Program as an additional major program within the National Bureau of Economic Research (NBER). The NBER is comprised of academics who study and report on various aspects of the U.S. economy. To date, this group has written only occasional papers about the nonprofit sector. By elevating the nonprofit sector to a standing program, this major economic activity could receive the attention that it merits.

The emphasis in recruiting NBER Research Associates and Faculty Research Fellows for such a nonprofit program should focus on the candidate's rigorous economic background accompanied by the highest levels of demonstrated academic excellence. The scholars' background and credentials in the philanthropic field should be weighted only secondarily, as a subsidiary consideration.

Federal government funding, accompanied by only a low level of restricted private contributions, would help the NBER to maintain its historic "independence and flexibility in choosing research activities"[56] when studying the philanthropic field which seems, perhaps unwittingly, to have an inordinate ability to blunt the academic acumen, creativity and assertiveness normally demonstrated in the study of other economic areas.

*Conclusions.* Low expectations of those involved in charities and philanthropy, with regard to the gathering, analysis and reporting of giving data, on the part of academia, government and the press, lead to the present situation in which reliable giving data in useful formats is not being disseminated to the public. As a result, the public cannot meaningfully evaluate its own giving patterns.

Low expectations of those involved in charities and philanthropy may be based both in an intrinsic cultural bias toward not expecting charitable data to be examined rigorously, as well as philanthropy not being perceived as an important financial sector of American society, in comparison to business and government. A third complicating, though not insurmountable, factor has to do with the fact that religion, which comprises a large portion of individual giving, is not required to report its finances, due to the constitutionally-based separation of church and state.

Yet, assuming the total nonprofit sector commands eight percent of the gross national product, the sector totaled about $650 billion in 1997.[57] Private support may amount to some 20 percent of the nonprofit total,[58] thus representing a substantial portion.

It has been suggested that between $6 trillion to $25 trillion may be bequeathed to charities over the next 50 years, out of a total $41 trillion to $136 trillion that is estimated will have changed hands over the next 50 years.[59]

These possibilities—along with the facts that (1) as of 1995, $227 billion was held in assets by foundations, an amount which one observer estimated

---

[56] "Support of the NBER," *National Bureau of Economic Research* (Cambridge, MA: National Bureau of Economic Research, n.d.), 8.

[57] The estimate that the total nonprofit sector commands 8% of the gross national product is derived as follows. *The Nonprofit Almanac 1996-1997* (San Francisco: Jossey-Bass, 1996), 4, states that "Total annual funds - independent sector" were $508.5 and $568.4 billion for 1992 and 1994 (preliminary), respectively. These estimates divided by the GNP of $6,255.5 and $6,955.2 billion for 1992 and 1994, respectively (*Statistical Abstract of the United States*, 1998, 456), yield a nonprofit sector estimate, as a percent of GNP, of 8.14% and 8.17% for 1992 and 1994, respectively. Multiplying 8.1% by the 1998 *Statistical Abstract*'s 1997 GNP figure of $8,060.1 billion yields $652.9 billion. This $652.9 billion estimate is consistent with the statement that

"total revenues to the non-profit world were more than $650 billion," by Mark R. Kramer in an article entitled "Grant Makers Shouldn't Play With Matches," in the November 18, 1999 issue of *Chronicle of Philanthropy*, 45.

[58] *Giving USA 1999*'s total $157.69 estimate of giving was adjusted to $134.44 billion by substituting *The State of Church Giving through 1997*'s 1997 estimate of Religion for *Giving USA 1999*'s 1997 estimate of Religion. The adjusted $134.44 billion estimate of 1997 total giving was divided by the estimated $650 billion nonprofit sector total to yield an estimated private support of 20.7% as a percentage of the nonprofit sector total.

[59] Thomas J. Billitteri, "Study: Charitable Bequests Could Total $25-Trillion During Next 50 Years," *Chronicle of Philanthropy*, November 4, 1999, 10.

as high as $400 billion[60] as of 1998, and (2) greater societal emphasis is being placed on the role the private sector, including faith-based organizations, plays in addressing various needs— suggest the value of greater academic attention to assessing, reporting and interpreting what giving levels actually are.

Of particular importance is gaining a valid measure over time of individual giving by sector. This measure will help Americans track the philanthropic impulse broadly, and more accurately assess longer-term trends. Such measurement is not impossible. For example, a model for reliable estimates of individual giving exists in the area of higher education.

The study of philanthropy would greatly benefit from an academic focus on accuracy using reported data with an eye toward historical trends, rather than on obtaining projections of the most recent year's data for use by commercial enterprises. Also, philanthropic information would improve if data for individual giving, from surveys or other IRS tax statistics, were tested against Form 990 reports.

To obtain improved information, it may be that much greater distance is needed between the practitioners of philanthropy and the academic research and study of philanthropic data.

Cultural observers from Alexis de Tocqueville forward have suggested the importance of religion and other volunteer societies for the development of a vibrant democracy within the United States. Adequate measures of individual giving over time within each of ten or so major charitable categories, will assist the public in understanding and evaluating their collective behavior.

---

[60] Claude N. Rosenberg, Jr., "Sharing the Wealth," *The American Benefactor*, Spring, 1998, 31

## chapter 8

# The Future of
# Congregational Giving:
# The Need for Creative Church Policy

During one of the longest economic expansions in the history of the U.S., church members did not increase the portion of income they gave to their churches. Why not?

Previous chapters in this volume document an overall decline since the 1960s in church giving as a percentage of income.

An obvious question is, Why has giving gone down?

Yet, a corollary development has not been explored in depth: (1) Members gave a smaller portion of their incomes to their churches during a time of sustained economic development. (2) Therefore, the church did not attract a larger portion of people's increasing resources; why not? It is this latter issue—why people did not increase giving when they had more resources at their disposal—that will be the main focus of this chapter.

A variety of reasons may help explain a decrease in giving as a percentage of income from the 1960s to the 1990s. For example, changes in American culture contributed to the decline. Consider that women going into the workforce meant less education about giving and missions was going on in the church. Global independence movements and increased communications confused many church members about the need to invest in international church programs that traditionally raised their commitment beyond their own needs.

Another aspect of the change in giving is that members did not increase the percentage of income donated, even though incomes were expanding. From this viewpoint, one concludes that the church did not effectively communicate a reason for members to donate to church programs more of their increased affluence.

Current church policy emphasizes two main reasons for members to make significant gifts to the church. One is endowments. The other is buildings. Regardless of rhetoric, church members are offered the preservation and upkeep of their institutions as a priority for giving. Church giving data demonstrates that this line of approach attracted a limited increase in dollars over the past three decades. Since the growth in income exceeded the growth in giving levels, the portion of income invested in the church decreased as a consequence.

Church leaders could offer a fresh and compelling vision for impacting world need in Jesus' name, and thereby increase giving. Immediate investment in global need—rather than establishing endowment funds that will meet those needs over time—has the advantage of providing prompt feedback to donors, thus encouraging additional giving among a broad base of church members.

Further, endowments, while historically useful, may belong to an earlier paradigm. A new model that is more responsive to the major economic changes in American society is needed.

To date, the assumption has been that endowments are the more effective means to meet needs than the immediate distribution of gifts. In this chapter, a mathematical model is presented that compares the results of the endowment approach with the results of immediate distribution. This model demonstrates that investing immediately in human beings may have more long-term benefits than building up endowment funds, even if the purpose of those endowments is also mission funding. A moratorium on gifts to endowments with a renewed focus on "endowing" human beings presently alive might provide an alternative agenda that will increase giving.

Finally, a strategy is outlined to strengthen congregations. By challenging wealthier members to match increased missions outreach through their congregations, the higher-income donor can leverage his/her giving by mobilizing church members who now give nothing, or only token amounts.

# NARRATIVE_____

*Why Has Giving Gone Down?* Previous chapters in this volume analyze church giving data that indicates members were giving a smaller portion of income to their congregations in the 1990s than in the late 1960s.

Other research suggests that giving has declined to churches for a variety of reasons. Some of these developments are documented in *Behind the Stained Glass Windows: Money Dynamics in the Church.*[61] The following discussion in this section is based on findings presented in that book.

Practical handicaps provide part of the explanation. For example, pastors are not trained to talk about money, from either a theological or administrative viewpoint.[62] Church members do not have effective training about money as a result.

Paradigmatic shifts—or changes in the very framework of the present worldview—have also affected giving. Women are now in the workforce and have less time to volunteer as stewardship and mission educators. The impact of this change is significant. A general consensus exists that women were largely the mission trainers in the congregation.[63] These promotion activities encouraged grassroots philanthropy education. With fewer women available to provide an ongoing educational emphasis on the broader responsibilities of the faith, a communications void developed in the church that has not yet been filled. Global mission was one commitment that raised members' visions beyond their own immediate needs. Without women actively involved in raising the sights of the congregation, a "club" mentality developed among the membership.

This situation was aggravated by communications technology. The whole world became so immediate that the average American found it overwhelming: This week, a disaster in the Philippines may be broadcast into living rooms; next week it will be an African nation. As Henri Nouwen and his coauthors observed, it is not that people have too little information, but rather too much. Feeling overwhelmed may easily lead people to feeling numb about the larger world in which they live.[64] With the needs of the neighbor blurring into an unapproachable composite disaster, religion is tempted to emphasize making people happy, rather than transforming them to be of service to others.

This communications overload produced by new technological advances occurred at the same time that traditional national church mission policy fell apart. On a de facto level, colonialism functioned as a framework in which most denominational, and even many parachurch, mission agencies pursued their goals. When global independence movements unraveled the strategy inherent in the geographical spheres of influence defined by colonialism, church leaders did not develop an alternative comprehensive plan. As a consequence, church members now felt responsible not for a particular region of the world, but for the whole of the increasingly complicated world. A new level of isolationism appeared as a tempting alternative.

The Cold War provided a framework for a while, dividing many mission agencies into camps, on one side of the issues or the other. One of the repercussions that accompanied the end of that political struggle was that the church was again left without a comprehensive missions approach.

The solution, of course, would not include a return to the destructive patterns of colonialism. However, creative thinking about how to interpret world need as part of one's faith commitment, in light of the changed circumstances, was not forthcoming from church leaders.

*Why Hasn't Church Giving Gone Up?* The issue of why giving has gone down has been widely discussed.

Another important issue generally escapes the attention of those concerned with the area of philanthropic behavior. The question can be asked, With the tremendous affluence that has spread through most levels of U.S. society in the decades since World War II, why hasn't giving to churches increased dramatically?

---

[61] John Ronsvalle and Sylvia Ronsvalle, *Behind the Stained Glass Windows: Money Dynamics in the Church* (Grand Rapids, MI: Baker Books, 1996).

[62] See the discussion in Ronsvalle and Ronsvalle, *Behind the Stained Glass Windows*, chapter 7, especially pages 140-152.

[63] Ronsvalle and Ronsvalle, *Behind the Stained Glass Windows*, 272.

[64] Donald McNeill, Douglas Morrison and Henri Nouwen, *Compassion* (New York: Doubleday, 1983), 53.

The tremendous potential for increased giving that is now present in American society has been all but invisible in our culture.

The biblical mandate to give money, whether the tithe (Matthew 23:23), or selling all one has and giving to the poor (Luke 12:33),[65] makes it safe to assume that positive giving patterns are to be expected among a well-functioning church. One would expect people successfully pursuing a faith walk to be increasing, rather than decreasing, the portion of income given to the church, particularly during times of economic growth. Therefore, the fact that it would be a positive development if giving increased to the church will be regarded as an operative understanding during this discussion.

While it may be tempting to look for where to place blame for declining donations, that approach is of limited value. Rather, a clear articulation of the problem might be more helpful in formulating solutions.

Such an articulation requires clear definitions. A brief review of a few basic concepts in behavioral psychology may be helpful here.

In Psychology 101 courses, students are taught to separate verbal statements from actual behaviors. For example, a heavy man may complain bitterly that he hates his weight. Yet, at dinner that night, the man orders and consumes an extra piece of pie. Should he have done that? What impact will his behavior have on his ability to get a date? Why would he do such a thing? None of these ideas is relevant from a behavioral viewpoint. Setting moral judgments aside, the only observation that can be made in the present context is that the man found the piece of pie more "reinforcing" than the discomfort of carrying his present weight. A layperson might translate this idea as, He wanted the pie more than he wanted to lose weight.

Applying this approach to church giving, some conclusions also are evident. First, church leaders say they want giving to go up. While church members provide a few more dollars in response, over the years incomes increase faster. As a result, member donations actually represent a smaller portion of the members' available resources in the 1990s than in the 1960s,

even though total resources have expanded. The observation can be made that the present behavior of church leaders does not produce the desired end result of increased giving by members.

Again, apart from moral judgments, two additional conclusions can be drawn. First, church members did not choose to spend a larger portion of their incomes on church activities.[66] Second, church leaders did not effectively communicate a reason for increasing donations such that members increased, rather than decreased, the portion of income given to the church.

It is important that the second conclusion is not read as a values statement. Assuming there is sincere interest in reversing current negative giving trends on the part of church leaders, a first step in developing a solution is to state clearly what is happening. Fault-finding is not the agenda. Should church members have given more because it is the right thing to do? Should church leaders have been more effective communicators? These issues are not immediately relevant in the present discussion. The observable facts are that members did not increase giving as a portion of income over the past three decades, and that church leaders did not effectively attract increased giving from members for the agenda that the leaders presented.

What behavior has defined church leaders' efforts to improve member giving? Two agendas are key components of the church's current approach.

***Current Church Policy: Institutional Maintenance.*** Two strategies serve as the de facto policy of church leaders to increase giving to the church. Whether the discussion occurs at the local, regional, or national level, church policy to increase giving is to ask for gifts for endowments and/or buildings. Any incipient endeavors to increase mission giving are seen to compete with the basic operations of the congregation, including the pastor's salary. That conflict is generally not acknowledged. In practice, missions funding is therefore treated passively while efforts to enhance the operations base through buildings and endowments are actively pursued.

**Endowments.** Endowments can be dedicated to a variety of purposes. An endowment might be for

---

[65] It should be noted that this particular pronouncement was not made by Jesus in the context of his encounter with the rich man. Rather, it is part of a general teaching session, introduced with the words, "Then Jesus said to his disciples" in Luke 12:22.

[66] As the discussion in chapter seven indicates, data does not support the idea that philanthropic activity other than the church has absorbed the difference between previous and current levels of church giving. Apart from any reallocation within giving levels, the present discussion is focused on why church giving has not increased.

the upkeep of the physical plant, for the operations of the congregation, or even for the mission work of the church. Endowments are seen as a way to secure the work of the church for the future. These accounts can absorb large gifts. The money received can be invested so that the balance increases over the years. The attraction of endowments may be the power that is associated with growing resources, independent of future unknowns (apart from fluctuations in the stock market). Endowments are emphasized in denominations such as the Presbyterian Church (U.S.A.) and The United Methodist Church, as well as independent "megachurches." Yet, these endowments have not had a significant positive impact on general giving patterns as a portion of income. Leaders voice support for endowments because these funds can secure the program or building of the church in the face of decreasing future support. What appears as a strength to leaders may communicate a siege mentality to potential donors.

**Buildings.** The other de facto policy offered by church leaders is to construct buildings. One church consultant suggested that a congregation ought to have some portion of a building under construction at all times, because people will give to a building, and the budget will be raised as a side benefit.[67] The focus on buildings is consistent with the "felt-needs" approach that emphasizes the church's responsiveness to the needs of the members.[68] All too quickly, this idea can move toward a consumer-approach to religion, emphasizing satisfied "customers" rather than the transformation of people into disciples. William Willimon reflected on this trend when he wrote,

> As William Sloane Coffin once asked, how can we attract people to the church by appealing to their self-centeredness and selfishness and then offer them the Christ who said that we find our lives by losing them, and that in dying we live?[69]

**Is the present church building boom unusual?** As a brief aside, the current level of building activity among churches in the U.S. has attracted attention in the media. Once again, data helps evaluate whether the present level of church construction exceeds that of past decades.

Census Bureau data indicates that new construction of religious buildings was about $1 billion dollars in 1964, compared to over $6.4 billion in 1998. So on a current-dollar level, more building was going on in the late 1990s than in the mid-1960s.

However, as has been emphasized in previous chapters of this volume, aggregate numbers considered apart from population, inflation, and changes in income, do not give a complete picture.

When inflation and population were taken into account, the data indicated that building in 1997 and 1998 was a little lower than during 1964-1966. In 1965, per capita expenditure in the U.S. on religious buildings was $26 dollars per person in inflation-adjusted 1992 dollars. In 1998, it was $21 dollars. Of course, a smaller portion of the entire U.S. population may have been investing in religious buildings in the late 1990s than in the mid-1960s. To have a meaningful comparison, changes in membership as a portion of population would have to be taken into account. Data considered in chapter five of this report suggests that membership in historically Christian churches declined as a portion of the U.S. population between 1968 and 1997. However, other religions were added to the religious milieu of the United States during this period. The Census data includes all religious construction, not just Christian churches. So the rough estimate may be fairly useful as a first approximation.

What may be more informative, however, is religious construction as a portion of income. Again, the $26 per capita spent on religious buildings in 1965 represented a different portion of income than the $21 spent in 1998. In fact, as a portion of income, Americans spent .26% on the construction of new buildings in 1965, compared to .11% in 1998.

The building activity occurring in the late 1990s has to be evaluated in the context of the general affluence produced by decades of economic expansion in the U.S.

**The care and feeding of the institution.** Both the endowment approach and the building approach emphasize the maintenance and care of the institution. Whether it is a place to meet, with offices in which to conduct business, or the larger operations structure of the church, leaders are communicating a goal that members should help the leaders to preserve themselves, albeit with the mitigating reason being to serve others.

---

[67] Ronsvalle and Ronsvalle, *Behind the Stained Glass Windows*, 51.

[68] For a discussion of the impact on the "felt-needs" approach on giving patterns, see *Behind the Stained Glass*

*Windows*, chapter two, especially pp. 41-47.

[69] William H. Willimon, "Will It Sell?," *The Christian Ministry*, November-December 1999, 47.

While endowments and buildings have attracted gifts of sometimes dramatic sizes, the overall portion of income donated to the church has continued to decline in general. It may therefore be observed that the present endowment/building policy has not effectively communicated a reason to the majority of church members to increase the portion of income given to the church.

***Endowing Institutions Versus Endowing Human Beings.*** *Behind the Stained Glass Windows* presents the findings from empty tomb, inc.'s multiyear Stewardship Project.[70] The Stewardship Project National Advisory Committee consisted of national representatives of fifteen communions and a seminary vice president. This group developed seven statements that the participants could agree on, even though the communions they represented spanned the theological spectrum. Having reviewed the observations and conclusions drawn from the Stewardship Project activities, the sixth conclusion reads: "The church needs a positive agenda for the great affluence in our society."[71] The assumption is that the church has a responsibility to help members integrate their ability to earn money with the practice of their faith. The church ought to provide members with a reason to spend more money on activities that are perceived as furthering God's work.

A related assumption is that if church leaders could help people integrate their money with their faith, church members would be willing to give more. Further, the process of giving more would have a positive impact on the practice of the individual's faith, and benefit the giver as much as the work of the church institution receiving the donation.

**A positive agenda.** What might a positive agenda look like?

Such an agenda would likely involve helping other human beings at their point of need. This idea is not only based on a theological mandate. Consider the outpouring of donations that result when a hurricane strikes a community in the U.S., or pictures of famine-stricken people in another country are broadcast into American living rooms.

Therefore, for the sake of the present discussion, suppose a positive agenda were proposed of stopping global child deaths in Jesus' name. The facts are that some 30,000 children under five die daily around the globe, for a total of 11.6 million a year. Further, most of these children are dying from preventable poverty conditions. One estimate suggested that $2.5 billion a year, carefully applied, could stop most of these deaths.[72]

So, suppose the goal of stopping child deaths in Jesus' name is offered as a compelling positive agenda for an increased portion of the affluence available to most church members.

**Comparing models to meet the need.** Given present church policy, it might be assumed that the most efficient way to meet this need would be to set up an endowment to accept these additional funds. This endowment would not only accept the funds in the first place, but the gifts would be invested to build up additional funds to help children in the future as well. Church leaders do not need to be sold on the value of compounding interest and capital gains.

Yet, in light of declining giving trends, this long-term approach has at least two drawbacks. First, church members are not given an immediate dynamic to attract their giving. Helping children who are not yet born might be logical, but it is not satisfying. One observation strongly affirmed in the Stewardship Project survey was that people want to know what their donated money is doing.[73] To date, money sitting in an account accumulating interest has not proved attractive enough to reverse present patterns.

The other drawback to the long-term investment approach is that the children who are born now, and need the help now, will not receive assistance now, the reason being that careful planning by those managing the funds values their existence less than preparing to help their counterparts who are not yet born.

Both of these reservations are emotional rather than factual. Therefore, a mathematical model was developed to explore, and objectify the discussion as to, whether the endowment approach is more beneficial than giving the money away as soon as it is received.

**Components of the mathematical model.** The mathematical model compared two strategies.

In both strategies, a basic assumption was made that money "invested" in a human being through meeting a need (particularly if done in Jesus' name,

---

[70] The full name of the project was Congregation-Level Field Observations and Denominational Giving Reports Stewardship Analysis Project, funded with a three-year grant from the Lilly Endowment Inc.

[71] Ronsvalle and Ronsvalle, *Behind the Stained Glass Windows*, 293.

[72] These facts are from UNICEF documents.

[73] Ronsvalle and Ronsvalle, *Behind the Stained Glass Windows*, 90.

although a weighting component for this factor was not calculated as part of the model) would "compound" the value of the initial investment in an ongoing fashion.

Placing the donations to help the children in an endowment might be termed the "Deferred" strategy. In this approach, $100 million is placed in an endowment fund. The average annual return was calculated at 8% over 50 years. Of the 8% each year, 3% was reinvested in the fund and compounded over the remaining portion of the 50 years. The other 5% was "invested" in human beings each year, with a compounded "return" rate of 8% a year.

For purposes of this model, the same percentage of return for the endowment fund was placed on healthy children. For example, one might assume that a child in whom blindness was prevented would compound her or his "value" to the global community at 8% a year. Some individuals helped as children might "produce" an even greater value to the global community than 8% a year. Yet, theologically, how can one calculate the "annual rate of return" of helping any child, in general, or a young Billy Graham or Mother Teresa, in particular, to grow up healthy and live to fulfill the individual's potential? Even so, for purposes of the present model, an average figure of 8% was used, a number similar to a somewhat conservative expectation for cash invested in the stocks and bonds market.[74]

Giving the money away immediately to help dying children might be termed the "Current" strategy. In this approach, the $100 million was immediately "invested" in helping human beings in Jesus' name. As noted above, the model calculated the "return" on this immediate investment in human beings at 8%, compounded annually.

The results are presented in Table 18.

**Table 18:** Financial Results of the "Deferred" Strategy and the "Current" Strategy

| Factor Description | "Deferred" Strategy | "Current" Strategy |
|---|---|---|
| Initial Investment | $100 million invested in endowment fund, with 8% annual return. Starting with Year 2, 3% reinvested in the endowment and compounded at 8% a year; 5% is "invested" in human beings, compounded at 8% a year. | $100 million "invested" in helping dying children in Jesus' name through church agencies. |
| Year 2 | | 2060% more "compounded investment" from the help given to dying children in Jesus' name. |
| Year 50 | | 11% more "compounded investment" from the help given to dying children in Jesus' name. |
| 50-Year Average | | 152% higher annual average "compounded investment" from the help given to dying children in Jesus' name. |
| Fund status as of Year 50 | $3.9 billion "compounded investment" in dying children (including actual "investment" of $564 million and compounded growth over 50 years) plus retained principal of $425.6 million in fund. | $4.3 billion "compounded investment" in dying children (including actual "investment" of $100 million and compounded growth over 50 years). |

[74] The authors overcame any reluctance to set the "value" of a healthy child at the same rate as endowment earnings, in part, by realizing that present behavior in the church, which tolerates the daily deaths of children around the globe, effectively values these children's lives at zero. A model that places increased value on children's lives might help raise awareness of their plight. Perhaps this thinking will also assist the reader.

**Observations about the results of the mathematical model.** Table 18 presents a number of noteworthy points.

If the number of dollars is valued, more money is actually "invested" in human beings in the "Deferred" Strategy over 50 years than in the "Current" Strategy. Over the 50 years, $564 million is shared with dying children in need in the Deferred Strategy, compared to $100 million in the Current Strategy.

However, the compounding aspect minimizes this difference. The children benefited by the "investment" from the Current Strategy continue to produce compounded "returns" over the entire 50-year period. By the end of the 50 years, at $4.3 billion invested in helping human beings, overall the immediate investment returned an annual average of 152% more benefit to humans in need than did the endowment model. Table 19 below presents the data in the comparison between the Deferred and Current Strategies.

It may also be noted that both strategies provide immediate "investment" in human beings. The immediate benefits of helping dying children is understood. However, the Deferred Strategy provides an additional form of human investment. In order to produce an 8% return on the money invested in the endowment fund, that money is invested in financially better-off persons, as available capital for businesses to use to produce more wealth.

Additional factors can also be considered in evaluating the strategies. For example, both strategies provide financial means for making a significant impact on the situations faced by dying children.

The two strategies, however, produce different designs for adapting to changing circumstances. In the Deferred Strategy, the donors retain control of most of the donated money, and can change how the money is used over the 50 years. In the Current strategy, the human beings who benefited from the immediate "investment" in them will be the ones who use the compounding "returns" in their lives to adapt to changing circumstances over 50 years.

The two strategies also may have a different effect on church members, who are another beneficiary of the plans. If these church members will benefit from integrating their faith and their money, then how the strategies encourage church members to increase giving should also be evaluated.

In the Deferred Strategy, the congregation is presented with a two-track model. Talented people will be needed to create and manage the endowment fund to insure an 8% return each year. Talented people will also be needed to interpret, educate, communicate, and inspire other members about the "investment" in the dying children.

In the Current Strategy, the congregation is presented with a one-track model. All the talented people in the congregation are asked to focus on the task of interpretation, education, communication, and inspiration of other members about the "investment" in the dying children.

The advantages of this single track should be understood. Many times, the most accomplished members of the congregation focus their talents on the task of creating and overseeing endowments. The members of the congregation who are successful in business have generally demonstrated real talent in their non-church life in the areas of leadership, creativity, and organization. The congregation's stewardship and mission education efforts might well benefit from these abilities if these talented people were not absorbed in directing endowment activities, and instead applied their personal gifts and experience by joining other members in mission interpretation.

Also, a message is sent to congregation members in general by the Deferred Strategy that the goal of future security is as important as helping dying children immediately. The Current strategy emphasizes the goal of helping dying children immediately.

Investing the $100 million gift in an endowment through the Deferred Strategy may also communicate a "ceiling" on the level of generosity needed. In contrast, the $100 million gift invested through the Current Strategy in immediate assistance to dying children might be seen as encouraging increased giving in an ongoing process.

Were church members to act on their potential for giving, then, an endowment might not be the most practical instrument to absorb the great amount of money donated annually. Instead, the task would shift, the goal being to provide donors with the means to keep sharing significant amounts of money each year to make an immediate difference. Endowments may be a strategy to manage money when expectations for the practice of continued good stewardship are low within congregations and denominations. When it is reasonable to assume that a broad base of church members are in a position to donate significant amounts for identifiable needs on a continuing basis, the task shifts from securing a fixed amount to build up over a period of years, to finding effective ways to share the funds generously donated on an ongoing basis.

78

**Table 19:** Deferred Strategy and Current Strategy, A Comparison of an Initial Investment of $100,000,000

| Year | Deferred Strategy: Cumulative Balance: $100,000,000 Endowment Fund with 3% reinvested | Deferred Strategy: Cumulative Balance: 5% "endowing" human beings, with 8% annually compounding benefit from "endowed" humans | Current Strategy: Cumulative Balance: $100,000,000 "endowing" human beings Year 1, with 8% annually compounding benefit from "endowed" humans | "Endowment" of Humans: Percent Difference of Current Strategy Compared to Deferred Strategy |
|---|---|---|---|---|
| 1 | $100,000,000 | | $100,000,000 | |
| 2 | $103,000,000 | $5,000,000 | $108,000,000 | 2060% |
| 3 | $106,090,000 | $10,550,000 | $116,640,000 | 1006% |
| 4 | $109,272,700 | $16,698,500 | $125,971,200 | 654% |
| 5 | $112,550,881 | $23,498,015 | $136,048,896 | 479% |
| 6 | $115,927,407 | $31,005,400 | $146,932,808 | 374% |
| 7 | $119,405,230 | $39,282,203 | $158,687,432 | 304% |
| 8 | $122,987,387 | $48,395,040 | $171,382,427 | 254% |
| 9 | $126,677,008 | $58,416,013 | $185,093,021 | 217% |
| 10 | $130,477,318 | $69,423,144 | $199,900,463 | 188% |
| 11 | $134,391,638 | $81,500,862 | $215,892,500 | 165% |
| 12 | $138,423,387 | $94,740,513 | $233,163,900 | 146% |
| 13 | $142,576,089 | $109,240,923 | $251,817,012 | 131% |
| 14 | $146,853,371 | $125,109,001 | $271,962,373 | 117% |
| 15 | $151,258,972 | $142,460,390 | $293,719,362 | 106% |
| 16 | $155,796,742 | $161,420,170 | $317,216,911 | 97% |
| 17 | $160,470,644 | $182,123,620 | $342,594,264 | 88% |
| 18 | $165,284,763 | $204,717,042 | $370,001,805 | 81% |
| 19 | $170,243,306 | $229,358,644 | $399,601,950 | 74% |
| 20 | $175,350,605 | $256,219,501 | $431,570,106 | 68% |
| 21 | $180,611,123 | $285,484,591 | $466,095,714 | 63% |
| 22 | $186,029,457 | $317,353,914 | $503,383,372 | 59% |
| 23 | $191,610,341 | $352,043,700 | $543,654,041 | 54% |
| 24 | $197,358,651 | $389,787,713 | $587,146,365 | 51% |
| 25 | $203,279,411 | $430,838,663 | $634,118,074 | 47% |
| 26 | $209,377,793 | $475,469,727 | $684,847,520 | 44% |
| 27 | $215,659,127 | $523,976,194 | $739,635,321 | 41% |
| 28 | $222,128,901 | $576,677,246 | $798,806,147 | 39% |
| 29 | $228,792,768 | $633,917,871 | $862,710,639 | 36% |
| 30 | $235,656,551 | $696,070,939 | $931,727,490 | 34% |
| 31 | $242,726,247 | $763,539,442 | $1,006,265,689 | 32% |
| 32 | $250,008,035 | $836,758,909 | $1,086,766,944 | 30% |
| 33 | $257,508,276 | $916,200,024 | $1,173,708,300 | 28% |
| 34 | $265,233,524 | $1,002,371,440 | $1,267,604,964 | 26% |
| 35 | $273,190,530 | $1,095,822,831 | $1,369,013,361 | 25% |
| 36 | $281,386,245 | $1,197,148,184 | $1,478,534,429 | 24% |
| 37 | $289,827,833 | $1,306,989,351 | $1,596,817,184 | 22% |
| 38 | $298,522,668 | $1,426,039,891 | $1,724,562,558 | 21% |
| 39 | $307,478,348 | $1,555,049,215 | $1,862,527,563 | 20% |
| 40 | $316,702,698 | $1,694,827,070 | $2,011,529,768 | 19% |
| 41 | $326,203,779 | $1,846,248,370 | $2,172,452,150 | 18% |
| 42 | $335,989,893 | $2,010,258,429 | $2,346,248,322 | 17% |
| 43 | $346,069,589 | $2,187,878,598 | $2,533,948,187 | 16% |
| 44 | $356,451,677 | $2,380,212,365 | $2,736,664,042 | 15% |
| 45 | $367,145,227 | $2,588,451,938 | $2,955,597,166 | 14% |
| 46 | $378,159,584 | $2,813,885,355 | $3,192,044,939 | 13% |
| 47 | $389,504,372 | $3,057,904,162 | $3,447,408,534 | 13% |
| 48 | $401,189,503 | $3,322,011,714 | $3,723,201,217 | 12% |
| 49 | $413,225,188 | $3,607,832,126 | $4,021,057,314 | 11% |
| 50 | $425,621,944 | $3,917,119,956 | $4,342,741,899 | 11% |
| | | | Annual Average for Years 1 through 50: | 152% |

An additional practical comparison between the Deferred Strategy and the Current Strategy has to do with fulfilling the initial intent of the donors in giving the money. The Current Strategy provides for the immediate implementation of the desire to help dying children in Jesus' name, as noted in the example above. Numerous examples exist of changes in focus of endowment funds. Thus, within the Deferred Strategy, the possibility exists for people in the future to change the intent of the endowment, so that within the 50-year period, the funds will be used for purposes other than helping dying children in Jesus' name. In contrast, the Current Strategy insures the funds are applied as the donors intended.

Table 20 presents these comparisons in summary form.

There are factors to recommend both the Deferred Strategy and the Current Strategy. The authors acknowledge that in the present discussion, emphasis has been placed on the Current Strategy. They beg the reader's indulgence on this point, given the fact that the Current Strategy generally receives no serious attention as a valid alternative. Perhaps that is because the basic working assumption about money is that the best thing to do with it is to accumulate it.

The compelling nature of the value of accumulating money is so deeply ingrained that the concept is rarely, if ever, challenged. While it may be log.cal, the accumulation approach represented by endowments may also be dated. To use a popular word, the "paradigm"—or framework of operation—may have shifted, making endowments a less useful concept than in the past.

**Endowments reflect a past paradigm.** Previously, the economic reality was that the minority of people had affluence beyond their basic needs, and the majority of people were struggling for survival. In this situation, the amount of resources were limited to what a smaller class of individuals were willing, and had available, to share. Large gifts could be given, and invested for use over time. In this way, a relatively small group of people were able to make a gift, and not be expected to "carry" the larger population year after year.

Since World War II, the landscape has changed. Now, the majority of people in a number of societies,

**Table 20:** Comparison of the "Deferred" Strategy and the "Current" Strategy

| Factor Description | "Deferred" Strategy | "Current" Strategy |
|---|---|---|
| Use of original $100 million | Initially available to business to create additional wealth, and then "invested" in dying children. | Immediately "invested" in dying children. |
| Adaptability | Donor retains control to adapt to changing circumstances over 50 years. | Children benefited use their increased "capital" to adapt to changing circumstances over 50 years. |
| Agenda provided | Two tracks are presented: Talented people to direct the endowment investments; talented people to interpret and educate about need. | One track presented: All talented people apply their gifts to interpretation and education about need. |
| Priority | Emphasizes future security. | Emphasizes mobilizing money on a scale consistent with potential giving to help now. |
| Comprehensive Agenda | Offers a large-scale vision for meeting need over time. | Offers a large-scale vision for meeting need immediately. |
| Continuing agenda | Implies that responsibility shifts from a limited number of initial donors to money managers; implies a "ceiling" to the need for donations. | Implies that continuing involvement among a broad base of donors is needed in coming years; initial gift is a "floor" on which to build, asking donors for ongoing annual commitment. |
| Achieving original intent | Endowment focus can be changed by future generations, meaning that initial intent is not fully achieved. | Intention of helping dying children immediately achieved. |

including the United States, had more resources than required for basic needs. The responsibility for the general welfare of not only American society but global need could be spread among a larger portion of the population. More people could also share in the satisfaction of making an impact on their surroundings during their lifetimes.

This new circumstance requires a different communications approach, however. Instead of emphasizing "noblesse oblige" to a limited group of people, the message needs to be reinterpreted to a much broader audience. Even as the media and public held accountable the turn-of-the-century wealthy, such as the Rockefellers, Carnegies, and Vanderbilts, today the national media follow the giving patterns of Ted Turner, Bill and Melinda Gates, and George Soros.

But who is holding accountable the rest of the population, the multitude of citizens who now have increased resources? The vast majority of potential donors in the church continue to escape serious engagement. Moreover, on an individual basis, these people do not have the amount of wealth to "invest" in long-term concepts that are attractive to someone with a large amount to give at one time. It is through the combination of many smaller gifts that the current strength and potential power resides among the vast majority of church members.

In these new circumstances, a strategy that emphasizes ongoing commitment of smaller amounts from many people, rather than mainly occasional large sums from a few, would be a more useful strategy. Future security for institutional maintenance activities does not communicate as much to this larger group as does feedback about what money already given has been doing.

Further, smaller amounts can be given over many years. This ongoing commitment therefore has the power to transform the givers by establishing new life priorities, even while it has a positive impact on the receivers.

Endowments may still have their place in some situations.[75] As a general strategy for congregational and denominational life, endowments may not be as useful an approach as in the past. What is needed is a strategy that can effectively attract comparatively smaller donations from a larger group of people over a sustained period of time.

Those concerned with philanthropy might compare this new situation with the consequences of technological developments in the world of computers. The Internet is changing everything from investing patterns to book publishing, as a function of making formerly exclusive activities accessible to a broad audience. Philanthropy can also continue to evolve and adapt to a new environment where more people have the potential to be involved at increased levels. New tools can help philanthropy adapt.

**Leadership may define how donors respond.** Leaders may defend the present policy of asking for major gifts for endowments and buildings with the rationale that past results indicate that people will give to these two agendas. Two ideas recommend that this perspective be rethought.

First, it should be asked, is the present policy producing the desired results? Of course fund-raisers rejoice when a large gift is secured. However, overall declining giving patterns are not being impacted. Is the goal to raise a certain (limited, in light of potential) amount of money for specific needs? Or is the goal to mobilize the vast majority of givers, to increase their levels of investment in the work of the church in an ongoing fashion?

Second, church leaders may be restricting donors' generosity by how they define the need. The watershed Commission on Private Philanthropy and Public Needs produced reports over a period of years by the U.S. Treasury Department. Various papers reflecting on the content of the Commission's findings were also published. One such paper observed:

> There is the added reality, omitted by the Commission's report, that patterns of support reflect what *donees seek*, as well as what donors select. Churches do not seek large individual gifts as a pattern, especially for their operating purposes. Universities do seek very large individual gifts, not only for current

---

[75] Some activities are of such an abstract nature that endowments may provide a firm base for necessary activities. Education is one example. Research may be another. In its experience, empty tomb, inc. has found that current donations are not available to fund activities that would explore how to reverse long-term declining giving patterns. Unable to locate sufficient current funds, empty tomb, inc. is in the process of trying to establish an endowment to provide an ongoing base to further such research and development activities. It is interesting to note that in the commercial realm, the value of research and development is acknowledged, unlike in the nonprofit environment.

operations, but for capital and endowment purposes. Donee influence likewise affects bequests. It is too simplistic to attribute the patterns of objects of gifts only to the wishes of the donors[76] [italics in original].

Some congregations have now begun to follow the pattern of universities, and request relatively larger gifts for endowments. However, is the church as an institution different than a university or, for that matter, a museum? As Douglas John Hall has pointed out, the sustained vitality of the North American church has been seated in its need to convince the population over and over again that its program is worthy of support.[77] Perhaps it would be worthwhile, in light of continuing giving patterns, to consider a different approach to raising the overall portion of income given to the church other than by emphasizing endowments.

Also, as uncomfortable as the fact may be, the Current Strategy is consistent with a general Christian theological framework.

**Theological view of sharing.** The concept of the Christian as "steward" might benefit from a fresh review.

In Matthew 24:45-51, Jesus presents the model of the disciple as caretaker of the master's agenda. The wise steward not only takes care of the master's interests, but also makes sure that all members of the household receive food and care at the proper time. Jesus warns that if the master returns and finds that the steward has decided to use the master's resources for personal indulgence, causing suffering on the part of other members of the household, then the master will punish the wicked steward.

From within the faith perspective, parallels might be drawn between the parable imagery and the church in the U.S. Resources are entrusted to the Christian to pursue the larger agenda of loving the neighbor out of love for God. If (1) children in the "global household" are dying from preventable poverty conditions; and (2) expenditures for personal indulgence in the U.S. are growing while the portion of income given to the church declines; then, do not church leaders have a responsibility to call those stewards to accountability on behalf of the Master? Perhaps a concern for the spiritual well-being of their parishioners could help pastors overcome their fear

of the expected pressures that would result from bringing up the topic of money.

Part of the difficulty in not achieving church giving potential may also have to do with confusion about values. Hugh Magers, former Director of Stewardship and now Director of Evangelism for The Episcopal Church, suggested that people misunderstand what real "treasure" is. " 'Lay up for yourself treasure in heaven.' *We* human beings are the treasure. We can use our resources to nurture folk into Heaven. We have an opportunity to establish a deep appropriation of the faith. Instead of being in a world with starving babies, we have the opportunity to help there be well babies and to support a friend for eternity."[78] While the logic supporting endowments and the related accumulation is tempting, from a theological viewpoint the better goal might be to use available resources to meet today's needs, particularly when technological communications advances have helped to define present need so clearly.

Finally, how Christians handle money needs to be informed by biblical rather than cultural standards. The established approach to money is that the main goal is to accumulate it. This idea contrasts with the biblical focus of a God who gives. As described in John 3:16, God gave his Son, and the church was founded through this action. Giving, rather than accumulating, is the defining hallmark of the church.

*Strategy for a New Paradigm.* The current policy of the church, that has tried to attract increased giving through buildings and endowments, has not reversed negative giving trends during a multi-decade economic expansion. Many prognosticators suggest that an economic "correction" is inevitable. If they are correct, an urgency permeates the need for a fresh agenda to help church members integrate their faith and money, while they still have access to expanded resources.

A moratorium on additional gifts to congregational and denominational endowments may be the most constructive step that the church can take at this point. A distinction is being made here between money that currently sits in existing endowments, and additional contributions to existing or newly forming endowments. Money that has already been donated to endowments is not under discussion. However,

---

76 Max M. Fisher et al., "Commentary on Page 133," *Giving in America: Toward a Stronger Voluntary Sector* (n.p.: Commission on Private Philanthropy and Public Needs, 1975), 203.

77 Douglas John Hall, *The Stewards: A Biblical Symbol Come of Age* (New York: Friendship Press, 1982), 2-3.
78 Ronsvalle and Ronsvalle, *Behind the Stained Glass Windows*, 184-185.

additional gifts to existing endowments, and the creation of new endowments, would be suspended under this approach.

Jesus challenged his followers to sell what they have and give to the poor. This particular behavior has not been typical of church members in the United States. Past behavior demonstrates that it is difficult to fit in with Jesus' directions in regard to money already accumulated. However, could church members, at the congregational community of faith institutional level, make a commitment, beforehand, to be faithful with money not yet received, with money they do not yet possess? Could a commitment be made to sell or dispose of gifts to help the poor *before* those gifts have been received? In this way, the resolve to be faithful would take root before the sticky nature of money has had the opportunity to exert itself.

The focus would then shift from building future security to being faithful with present responsibility. Many smaller and larger gifts from many different people can be combined to impact current need, as a response to the Master's direction. The immediate feedback from "investment" in people in need will possibly have the positive effect of reinforcing giving behavior, and encourage ongoing giving.

**A game plan for the relatively wealthy to help revitalize the practice of philanthropy in congregations.** The present environment in which congregations exist requires a different approach from the traditional endowment and building strategy. One idea being developed by the authors is a "Matching" concept. Members who have accumulated a sizable amount of this world's goods could provide leadership that will help to revitalize the majority of people in congregations who are not presently engaged in faithful giving behavior. This game plan is built on three key ideas.

- Research by the authors has established that most congregations currently have a maintenance mentality. As 84% of the pastors and 89% of the regional officials responding to the Stewardship Project survey affirmed, "In most congregations, the goal of stewardship is defined as meeting the budget."[79] This maintenance mentality does not foster increased giving, and therefore needs to be addressed.

- The authors are not aware of nationwide quantitative research on the percentage of people who do not give to the local congregation. However, in discussion with denominational leaders across the theological spectrum, the idea that 30-50% of the resident members do not give anything to the local congregation has been affirmed. A plan to increase giving must engage those presently not involved in the practice.

- Again, lacking quantitative research, the authors have had the opportunity to talk with both church leaders and wealthy individuals about the idea of why wealthy people rarely tithe to their congregations. Repeatedly, the opinion was stated that well-to-do people often do not feel they have a good reason to invest sizable amounts of their money in a congregation. Reasons vary from not wanting to create a "welfare" mentality to not feeling the congregation is not doing anything significant enough to merit large donations.

If there were less of an emphasis on endowments or buildings, what might attract the increased financial participation of wealthier-than-average members in the life of the congregation?

The authors are currently testing a plan in their ongoing work with congregations. The first component is for the local congregation to establish a baseline for its present operations. The commitment is made that any money received beyond this baseline—including undesignated bequests, and increased giving—will be directed by the congregation to expand mission outreach, both globally and locally.

The second component of the plan is to secure commitments from one or more wealthier-than-average members in the congregation. The commitment is that this individual will first make a regular pledge to the baseline budget of the church. Chances are very good that this commitment will not represent 10% of this wealthy member's income. (It should be noted that a variety of church experts believe wealthy members should not be limited by the 10% guideline.) So the member is asked to make an additional commitment, up to a certain dollar figure defined by the wealthy individual, to match all money that is donated by the rest of the congregation beyond

---

[79] Ronsvalle and Ronsvalle, *Behind the Stained Glass Windows*, 121.

the baseline budget. The purpose of this additional money is to expand mission outreach.

This approach provides the well-to-do member with a reason to invest a greater portion of income in the congregation. The plan also emphasizes the need for *all* members of the congregation to first, secure the baseline budget of the congregation, and then, to exceed that budget in order to expand the global and local mission outreach of the congregation.

Information about the authors' work with congregations through The National Money for Missions Program is available at the Web site <www.emptytomb.org>.

***Summary.*** Present church policy, emphasizing buildings and endowments as a means to attract increased giving to the church, has not significantly reversed negative giving trends.

A mathematical model compared a "Deferred" Strategy, emphasizing endowment funds helping dying children, and a "Current" Strategy, emphasizing immediate help directed to dying children. The Current Strategy produced a higher annual average benefit in humans helped.

Endowments may be rooted in a paradigm that no longer defines present church circumstances. Broadly-distributed affluence has produced a majority of people in the society who have more resources than they require to meet their basic needs. A strategy that emphasizes immediate "investment" in meeting the needs of other human beings may be more useful in raising giving levels, than the endowment approach which emphasizes long-term investment and accompanying delayed response to need.

Biblically, an emphasis on giving, rather than accumulation, may also suggest that the Current Strategy will be more helpful in assisting church members in the United States to integrate their faith and money.

New strategies will be needed to attract increased donations, such as matching additional mission giving. Creative thinking may produce fresh initiatives, suited to the present cultural and economic environment, to reverse declining giving patterns in the church.

# APPENDIXES

# APPENDIX A: *List of Denominations*

## Church Member Giving, 1968-1997

American Baptist Churches in the U.S.A.
Associate Reformed Presbyterian Church
  (General Synod)
Brethren in Christ Church
Christian Church (Disciples of Christ)
Church of God (Anderson, Ind.)
Church of God General Conference (Oregon, IL and
  Morrow, GA.)
Church of the Brethren (through 1995)
Church of the Nazarene
Conservative Congregational Christian Conference
Cumberland Presbyterian Church
Evangelical Congregational Church
Evangelical Covenant Church
Evangelical Lutheran Church in America
  The American Lutheran Church (merged 1987)
  Lutheran Church in America (merged 1987)
Evangelical Lutheran Synod
Evangelical Mennonite Church
Fellowship of Evangelical Bible Churches
Free Methodist Church of North America
Friends United Meeting (through 1990)
General Association of General Baptists
Lutheran Church-Missouri Synod
Mennonite Church
Moravian Church in America, Northern Province
North American Baptist Conference
The Orthodox Presbyterian Church
Presbyterian Church (U.S.A.)
Reformed Church in America
Seventh-day Adventists
Southern Baptist Convention
United Church of Christ
Wisconsin Evangelical Lutheran Synod

## Church Member Giving, 1996–1997

The Denominations included in the 1968-1997
  analysis with data available for both years plus the
  following:
Allegheny Wesleyan Methodist Connection
  (Original Allegheny Conference)
Apostolic Faith Mission Church of God
Christian and Missionary Alliance
Church of Christ (Holiness) U.S.A.
Church of Lutheran Brethren of America
Church of the Lutheran Confession

Churches of God General Conference
The Episcopal Church
International Pentecostal Church of Christ
Missionary Church, Inc.
National Association of Free Will Baptists
Presbyterian Church in America
United Brethren in Christ, Church of
The United Methodist Church
The Wesleyan Church

## By Organizational Affiliation: NAE, 1968-1997

Brethren in Christ Church
Church of the Nazarene
Conservative Congregational Christian Conference
Evangelical Congregational Church
Evangelical Mennonite Church
Fellowship of Evangelical Bible Churches
Free Methodist Church of North America
General Association of General Baptists

## By Organizational Affiliation: NCC, 1968-1997

American Baptist Churches in the U.S.A.
Christian Church (Disciples of Christ)
Evangelical Lutheran Church in America
Moravian Church in America, Northern Province
Presbyterian Church (U.S.A.)
Reformed Church in America
United Church of Christ

## Eleven Denominations, 1921-1997

American Baptist (Northern)
Christian Church (Disciples of Christ)
Church of the Brethren
The Episcopal Church
Evangelical Lutheran Church in America
  The American Lutheran Church
    American Lutheran Church
    The Evangelical Lutheran Church
    United Evangelical Lutheran Church
    Lutheran Free Church
  Evangelical Lutheran Churches, Assn. of
  Lutheran Church in America
    United Lutheran Church
      General Council Evangelical Lutheran Ch.
      General Synod of Evangelical Lutheran Ch.

United Synod Evangelical Lutheran South
American Evangelical Lutheran Church
Augustana Lutheran Church
Finnish Lutheran Church (Suomi Synod)
Moravian Church in America, Northern Province
Presbyterian Church (U.S.A.)
United Presbyterian Church in the U.S.A.
Presbyterian Church in the U.S.A.
United Presbyterian Church in North America
Presbyterian Church in the U.S.
Reformed Church in America
Southern Baptist Convention
United Church of Christ
Congregational Christian
Congregational
Evangelical and Reformed
Evangelical Synod of North America/German
Reformed Church in the U.S.
The United Methodist Church
The Evangelical United Brethren
The Methodist Church
Methodist Episcopal Church
Methodist Episcopal Church South
Methodist Protestant Church

Cumberland Presbyterian Church
Evangelical Congregational Church
Evangelical Covenant Church
Evangelical Lutheran Synod
Evangelical Mennonite Church
Fellowship of Evan. Bible Churches
Free Methodist Church of North America
Friends United Meeting
General Association of General Baptists
Lutheran Church-Missouri Synod
Mennonite Church
North American Baptist Conference
The Orthodox Presbyterian Church
Salvation Army
Seventh-day Adventists
Southern Baptist Convention
Wisconsin Evangelical Lutheran Synod

## Trends in Membership, 10 Mainline Protestant Denominations, 1968-1997

American Baptist Churches in the U.S.A.
Christian Church (Disciples of Christ)
Church of the Brethren
The Episcopal Church
Evangelical Lutheran Church in Am.
Moravian Church in America, Northern Prov.
Presbyterian Church (U.S.A.)
Reformed Church in America
United Church of Christ
The United Methodist Church

## Trends in Membership, Add 27 Denominations, 1968-1997

Assemblies of God
Associate Reformed Presby. Ch (Gen Synod)
Baptist General Conference
Brethren in Christ Church
Christian and Missionary Alliance
Church of God (Anderson, IN)
Church of God (Cleveland, Tenn.)
Church of God, Gen. Conf. (Oregon, IL
  and Morrow, GA)
Church of the Nazarene
Conservative Cong. Christian Conf.

# APPENDIX B SERIES: *Denominational Data Tables*

## Introduction

The data in the following tables is from the *Yearbook of American and Canadian Churches* (*YACC*) series unless otherwise noted. Financial data is presented in current dollars.

Data in italics indicates a change from the previous edition in *The State of Church Giving* (SCG) series.

The Appendix B tables are described below.

*Appendix B-1, Church Member Giving, 1968-1997:* This table presents data for the denominations which comprise the data set analyzed for the 1968 through 1997 period.

Elements of this data are also used for the analyses in chapters two through seven.

In Appendix B-1, the data for the Presbyterian Church (U.S.A.) combined data for the United Presbyterian Church in the U.S.A. and the Presbyterian Church in the United States for the period 1968 through 1982. These two communions merged to become the Presbyterian Church (U.S.A.) in 1983, data for which is presented for 1983 through 1997.

Also in Appendix B-1, data for the Evangelical Lutheran Church in America (ELCA) appears beginning in 1987. Before that, the two major component communions that merged into the ELCA—the American Lutheran Church and the Lutheran Church in America—are listed as individual denominations from 1968 through 1986.

In the Appendix B series, the denomination listed as the Fellowship of Evangelical Bible Churches has been named the Evangelical Mennonite Brethren Church prior to July 1987.

Comments about the data for two denominations should be noted.

Data for the American Baptist Churches in the U.S.A. has been obtained directly from the denominational office as follows. In discussions with the American Baptist Churches Office of Planning Resources, it became apparent that there had been no distinction made between the membership of congregations reporting financial data, and total membership for the denomination, when reporting data to the Yearbook *of American and Canadian Churches*. Records were obtained from the denomination for a smaller membership figure that reflected only those congregations reporting financial data. While this revised membership data provided a more useful per member giving figure for Congregational Finances, the total Benevolences figure reported to the *YACC*, while included in the present data set, does reflect contributions to some Benevolences categories from 100% of the American Baptist membership. The membership reported in Appendix B-1 for the American Baptist Churches is the membership for congregations reporting financial data, rather than the total membership figure prided in editions of the *YACC*. However, in the sections that consider membership as a percentage of population, the Total Membership figure for the American Baptist Churches is used.

Data for the Southern Baptist Convention (SBC) included in *The State of Church Giving through 1997* are presented as reported in the Yearbook of American and Canadian Churches series, or obtained directly from the denomination. The past three editions in *The State of Church Giving* series included averaged SBC figures: Congregational Finances and Benevolences figures for data year 1994 (SCG94 and SCG95); and Congregational Finances for data year 1995 (*SCG96*). In correspondence about 1994 data, the SBC denominational office indicated that it was possible that the 1994 Congregational Finances data was artificially high, due to a change in reporting methodology. Therefore, in consultation with that office, figures for both Congregational Finances and Benevolences, averaged between 1993 and 1995, were used in *SCG94* and SCG95, to avoid what, at the time, seemed to have been an artificial decline from 1994 to 1995. However, when 1996 data became available, correspondence to the denominational office led to the conclusion that the 1994 data was not unusually high, but that the 1995 data was unusually low. Also, the question could be localized to the category of Congregational Finances. Therefore, an estimate for 1995 SBC Congregational Finances was obtained by averaging 1994 and 1996 data, and used in *SCG96*, while the 1994 data as reported to the *YACC* was used in *SCG96*. As of SCG97, it was decided for the present and future editions in the *SCG* series, that reported denominational data will not be adjusted in response to the possibility of unusual circumstances possibly affecting the data. Rather data will be presented as reported either in the *YACC* series or as obtained directly from the denomination.

***Appendix B-2, Church Member Giving, 1996-1997:*** Appendix B-2 presents the Full or Confirmed Membership, Congregational Finances and Benevolences data for the fifteen additional denominations included in the 1996-1997 comparison.

***Appendix B-3, Church Member Giving for Eleven Denominations, 1921-1997:*** This appendix presents additional data which is not included in Appendix B-1 for the Eleven Denominations.

The data from 1921 through 1928 in Appendix B-3.1 is taken from summary information contained in the *Yearbook of American Churches, 1949 Edition*, George F. Ketcham, ed. (Lebanon, PA: Sowers Printing Company, 1949, p. 162). The summary membership data provided is for Inclusive Membership. Therefore, giving as a percentage of income for the years 1921 through 1928 may have been somewhat higher had Full or Confirmed Membership been used. The list of denominations that are summarized for this period is presented in the *Yearbook of American Churches, 1953 Edition*, Benson Y. Landis, ed. (New York: National Council of the Churches of Christ in the U.S.A., 1953, p. 274).

The data from 1929 through 1952 is taken from summary information presented in the *Yearbook of American Churches, Edition for 1955*, Benson Y. Landis, ed. (New York: National Council of the Churches of Christ in the U.S.A., 1954, pp. 286-287). A description of the list of denominations included in the 1929 through 1952 data summary on page 275 of the *YACC Edition for 1955* indicated that the Moravian Church, Northern Province is not included in the 1929 through 1952 data.

The data in Appendix B-3.2 for 1953 through 1964 was obtained for the indicated denominations from the relevant edition of the *YACC* series. Giving as a percentage of income was derived for these years by dividing the published Total Contributions figure by the published Per Capita figure to produce a membership figure for each denomination. The Total Contributions figures for the denominations were added to produce an aggregated Total Contributions figure. The calculated membership figures were also added to produce an aggregated membership figure. The aggregated Total Contributions figure was then divided by the aggregated membership figure to yield a per member giving figure which was used in calculating giving as a percentage of income.

Data for the years 1965 through 1967 was not available in a form that could be readily analyzed for the present purposes, and therefore data for these three years was estimated by dividing the change in per capita Total Contributions from 1964 to 1968 by four, the number of years in this interval, and cumulatively adding the result to the base year of 1964 and the succeeding years of 1965 and 1966 to obtain estimates for the years 1965 through 1967.

In most cases, this procedure was also applied to individual denominations to avoid an artificially low total due to missing data. If data was not available for a specific year, the otherwise blank entry was filled in with a calculation based on surrounding years for the denomination. For example, this procedure was used for the American Baptist Churches for the years 1955 and 1996, the Christian Church (Disciples of Christ) for the years 1955 and 1959, and the Evangelical United Brethren, later to merge into The United Methodist Church, for the years 1957, 1958 and 1959. Data for the Methodist Church was changed for 1957 in a similar manner.

Available Total Contributions and Full or Confirmed Members data for The Episcopal Church and The United Methodist Church for 1969 through 1997 is presented in Appendix B-3.3. These two communions are included in the Eleven Denominations . The United Methodist Church was created in 1968 when the Methodist Church and the Evangelical United Brethren Church merged. While the Methodist Church filed summary data for the year 1968, the Evangelical United Brethren Church did not. Data for these denominations was calculated as noted in the appendix. However, since the 1968 data for The Methodist Church would not have been comparable to the 1985 and 1997 data for The United Methodist Church, this communion was not included in the more focused 1968-1997 analysis.

***Appendix B-4, Trends in Giving and Membership:*** This appendix presents denominational membership data used in the membership analyses presented in chapter five that is not available in the other appendices.

# APPENDIX B-1: *Church Member Giving 1968-1997*

Key to Denominational Abbreviations: Data Years 1968-1997

| Abbreviation | Denomination |
|---|---|
| abc | American Baptist Churches in the U.S.A. |
| alc | The American Lutheran Church |
| arp | Associate Reformed Presbyterian Church (General Synod) |
| bcc | Brethren in Christ Church |
| ccd | Christian Church (Disciples of Christ) |
| cga | Church of God (Anderson, IN) |
| cgg | Church of God General Conference (Oregon, IL) |
| chb | Church of the Brethren |
| chn | Church of the Nazarene |
| ccc | Conservative Congregational Christian Conference |
| cpc | Cumberland Presbyterian Church |
| ecc | Evangelical Congregational Church |
| ecv | Evangelical Covenant Church |
| elc | Evangelical Lutheran Church in America |
| els | Evangelical Lutheran Synod |
| emc | Evangelical Mennonite Church |
| feb | Fellowship of Evangelical Bible Churches |
| fmc | Free Methodist Church of North America |
| fum | Friends United Meeting |
| ggb | General Association of General Baptists |
| lca | Lutheran Church in America |
| lms | Lutheran Church-Missouri Synod |
| mch | Mennonite Church |
| mca | Moravian Church in America, Northern Province |
| nab | North American Baptist Conference |
| opc | The Orthodox Presbyterian Church |
| pch | Presbyterian Church (U.S.A.) |
| rca | Reformed Church in America |
| sda | Seventh-day Adventists |
| sbc | Southern Baptist Convention |
| ucc | United Church of Christ |
| wel | Wisconsin Evangelical Lutheran Synod |

Appendix B-1: Church Member Giving, 1968-1997 (continued)

| | Data Year 1968 | | | Data Year 1969 | | | Data Year 1970 | | |
|---|---|---|---|---|---|---|---|---|---|
| | Full/Confirmed Members | Congregational Finances | Benevolences | Full/Confirmed Members | Congregational Finances | Benevolences | Full/Confirmed Members | Congregational Finances | Benevolences |
| abc | 1,179,848 a | $95,878,267 a | $21,674,924 a | 1,153,785 a | $104,084,322 | $21,111,333 | 1,231,944 a | $112,668,310 | $19,655,391 |
| alc | 1,767,618 | 137,260,390 | 32,862,410 | 1,771,999 | 143,917,440 | 34,394,570 | 1,775,573 | 146,268,320 | 30,750,030 |
| arp | 28,312 a | 2,211,002 a | 898,430 a | 28,273 | 2,436,936 a | 824,628 a | 28,427 a | 2,585,974 a | 806,071 a |
| bcc | 8,954 | 1,645,256 | 633,200 a | 9,145 | 1,795,859 | 817,445 | NA | NA | NA |
| ccd | 994,683 | 105,803,222 | 21,703,947 | 936,931 | 91,169,842 | 18,946,815 | 911,964 | 98,671,692 | 17,386,032 |
| cga | 146,807 | 23,310,682 | 4,168,580 | 147,752 | 24,828,448 | 4,531,678 | 150,198 | 26,962,037 | 4,886,223 |
| cgg | 6,600 | 805,000 | 103,000 | 6,700 | 805,000 | 104,000 | 6,800 | 810,000 | 107,000 |
| chb | 187,957 | 12,975,829 | 4,889,727 | 185,198 | 13,964,158 | 4,921,991 | 182,614 | 14,327,896 | 4,891,618 |
| chn | 364,789 | 59,943,750 a | 14,163,761 a | 372,943 | 64,487,669 a | 15,220,339 a | 383,284 | 68,877,922 a | 16,221,123 a |
| ccc | 15,127 | 1,867,978 | 753,686 | 16,219 | 1,382,195 | 801,534 | 17,328 | 1,736,818 | 779,696 |
| cpc | 86,729 a | 5,542,678 a | 906,583 a | 88,091 | 6,393,665 | 1,020,248 | NA | NA | NA |
| ecc | 29,582 a | 3,369,308 a | 627,731 a | 29,652 a | 3,521,074 a | 646,187 a | 29,437 a | 3,786,288 a | 692,428 a |
| ecv | 66,021 | 14,374,162 a | 3,072,848 | 67,522 | 14,952,302 a | 3,312,306 | 67,441 | 15,874,265 a | 3,578,876 |
| elc | ALC & LCA | ALC & LCA | ALC & LCA | ALC & LCA | ALC & LCA | ALC & LCA | ALC & LCA | ALC & LCA | ALC & LCA |
| els | 10,886 a | 844,235 a | 241,949 a | 11,079 | 1,003,746 | 315,325 | 11,030 | 969,625 | 242,831 a |
| emc | 2,870 a | 447,397 | 232,331 | NA | NA | NA | NA | NA | NA |
| feb | 1,712 a | 156,789 a | 129,818 a | 3,324 | 389,000 | 328,000 | 3,698 | 381,877 | 706,398 |
| fmc | 47,831 a | 12,032,016 a | 2,269,677 a | 47,954 a | 9,152,729 | 7,495,653 | 64,901 | 9,641,202 | 7,985,264 |
| fum | 55,469 | 3,564,793 | 1,256,192 | 55,257 | 3,509,509 | 1,289,026 | 53,970 | 3,973,802 | 1,167,183 |
| ggb | 65,000 | 4,303,183 a | 269,921 a | NA | NA | NA | NA | NA | NA |
| lca | 2,279,383 | 166,337,149 | 39,981,858 | 2,193,321 | 161,958,669 | 46,902,225 | 2,187,015 | 169,795,380 | 42,118,870 |
| lms | 1,877,799 | 178,042,762 | 47,415,800 | 1,900,708 | 185,827,626 | 49,402,590 | 1,922,569 | 193,352,322 | 47,810,664 |
| mch | 85,682 a | 7,078,164 a | 5,576,305 a | 85,343 | 7,398,182 | 6,038,730 | 83,747 a | 7,980,917 a | 6,519,476 a |
| mca | 27,772 | 2,583,354 | 444,910 | 27,617 | 2,642,529 | 456,182 | 27,173 | 2,704,105 | 463,219 |
| nab | 42,371 a | 5,176,669 a | 1,383,964 a | 55,100 | 6,681,410 | 2,111,588 | 55,080 | 6,586,929 | 2,368,288 |
| opc | 9,197 | 1,638,437 | 418,102 | 9,276 | 1,761,242 | 464,660 | NA | NA | NA |
| pch | 4,180,093 | 375,248,474 | 102,622,450 | 4,118,664 | 388,268,169 | 97,897,522 | 4,041,813 | 401,785,731 | 93,927,852 |
| rca | 226,819 a | 25,410,489 a | 9,197,642 a | 224,992 a | 27,139,579 a | 9,173,312 a | 223,353 a | 29,421,849 a | 9,479,503 a |
| sda | 395,159 a | 36,976,280 | 95,178,335 | 407,766 | 40,378,426 | 102,730,594 | 420,419 | 45,280,059 | 109,569,241 |
| sbc | 11,332,229 a | 666,924,020 a | 128,023,731 a | 11,487,708 | 709,246,590 | 133,203,885 | 11,628,032 | 753,510,973 | 138,480,329 |
| ucc | 2,032,648 a | 152,301,536 | 18,869,136 | 1,997,898 | 152,791,512 | 27,338,543 | 1,960,608 | 155,248,767 | 26,934,289 |
| wel | 259,954 a | 19,000,023 a | 6,574,308 a | 265,069 | 20,786,613 | 6,417,042 | 271,117 | 22,582,545 | 6,810,612 |
| Total | 27,815,901 | $2,120,602,216 | $566,545,256 | 27,705,286 | $2,189,890,976 | $598,217,951 | 27,739,535 | $2,293,220,958 | $594,338,507 |

[a]Data obtained from denominational source.

| | Data Year 1971 | | | Data Year 1972 | | | Data Year 1973 | | |
|---|---|---|---|---|---|---|---|---|---|
| | Full/Confirmed Members | Congregational Finances | Benevolences | Full/Confirmed Members | Congregational Finances | Benevolences | Full/Confirmed Members | Congregational Finances | Benevolences |
| abc | 1,223,735 a | $114,673,805 | $18,878,769 | 1,176,092 a | $118,446,573 | $18,993,440 | 1,190,455 a | $139,357,611 | $20,537,388 |
| alc | 1,775,774 | 146,324,460 | 28,321,740 | 1,773,414 | 154,786,570 | 30,133,850 | 1,770,119 | 168,194,730 | 35,211,440 |
| arp | 28,443 a | 2,942,577 a | 814,703 a | 28,711 a | 3,329,446 a | 847,665 a | 28,763 a | 3,742,773 a | 750,387 a |
| bcc | 9,550 | 2,357,786 | 851,725 | 9,730 | 2,440,400 | 978,957 | NA | NA | NA |
| ccd | 884,929 | 94,091,862 | 17,770,799 | 881,467 | 105,763,511 | 18,323,685 | 868,895 | 112,526,538 | 19,800,843 |
| cga | 152,787 | 28,343,604 | 5,062,282 | 155,920 | 31,580,751 | 5,550,487 | 157,828 | 34,649,592 | 6,349,695 |
| cgg | 7,200 | 860,000 | 120,000 | 7,400 | 900,000 | 120,000 | 7,440 | 940,000 | 120,000 |
| chb | 181,183 | 14,535,274 | 5,184,768 | 179,641 | 14,622,319 b | 5,337,277 b | 179,333 | 16,474,758 | 6,868,927 |
| chn | 394,197 | 75,107,918 a | 17,859,332 a | 404,732 | 82,891,903 a | 20,119,679 a | 417,200 | 91,318,469 a | 22,661,140 a |
| ccc | 19,279 a | 1,875,010 a | 930,485 a | 20,081 a | 1,950,865 a | 994,453 a | 20,712 a | 2,080,038 a | 1,057,869 a |
| cpc | 57,147 | 6,848,115 | 1,139,480 | 56,212 | 8,449,593 | 554,843 | 56,584 | 9,715,351 | 847,727 |
| ecc | 29,682 a | 4,076,576 a | 742,293 a | 29,434 a | 4,303,406 a | 798,968 a | 29,331 a | 4,913,214 a | 943,619 a |
| ecv | 68,428 | 17,066,051 a | 3,841,887 | 69,815 | 18,021,767 a | 4,169,053 | 69,922 | 18,948,864 a | 4,259,950 |
| elc | ALC & LCA | ALC & LCA | ALC & LCA | ALC & LCA | ALC & LCA | ALC & LCA | ALC & LCA | ALC & LCA | ALC & LCA |
| els | 11,426 a | 1,067,650 a | 314,335 a | 11,532 | 1,138,953 | 295,941 a | 12,525 | 1,296,326 | 330,052 a |
| emc | NA | NA | NA | NA | NA | NA | 3,131 | 593,070 | 408,440 |
| feb | NA | NA | NA | NA | NA | NA | NA | NA | NA |
| fmc | 65,040 | 13,863,601 | 6,092,503 | 48,455 | 15,206,381 | 6,638,789 | 48,763 a | 17,483,258 | 7,000,353 |
| fum | 54,522 | 3,888,064 | 1,208,062 | 54,927 | 4,515,463 | 1,297,088 | 57,690 | 5,037,848 | 1,327,439 |
| ggb | NA | NA | NA | NA | NA | NA | NA | NA | NA |
| lca | 2,175,378 | 179,570,467 | 43,599,913 | 2,165,591 | 188,387,949 | 45,587,481 | 2,169,341 | 200,278,486 | 34,627,978 |
| lms | 1,945,889 | 203,619,804 | 48,891,368 | 1,963,262 | 216,756,345 | 50,777,670 | 1,983,114 | 230,435,598 | 54,438,074 |
| mch | 88,522 | 8,171,316 | 7,035,750 | 89,505 | 9,913,176 | 7,168,664 | 90,967 | 9,072,858 | 6,159,740 |
| mca | 26,101 | 2,576,172 | 459,447 | 25,500 | 2,909,252 | 465,316 | 25,468 | 3,020,667 | 512,424 |
| nab | 54,997 | 7,114,457 | 2,293,692 | 54,441 | 7,519,558 | 2,253,158 | 41,516 | 6,030,352 | 1,712,092 |
| opc | NA | NA | NA | NA | NA | NA | NA | NA | NA |
| pch | 3,963,665 | 420,865,807 | 93,164,548 | 3,855,494 | 436,042,890 | 92,691,469 | 3,730,312 c | 480,735,088 c | 95,462,247 c |
| rca | 219,915 a | 32,217,319 a | 9,449,655 a | 217,583 | 34,569,874 a | 9,508,818 a | 212,906 a | 39,524,443 a | 10,388,619 a |
| sda | 433,906 | 49,208,043 | 119,913,879 | 449,188 | 54,988,781 | 132,411,980 | 464,276 | 60,643,602 | 149,994,942 |
| sbc | 11,824,676 | 814,406,626 | 160,510,775 | 12,065,333 | 896,427,208 | 174,711,648 | 12,295,400 | 1,011,467,569 | 193,511,983 |
| ucc | 1,928,674 | 158,924,956 | 26,409,521 | 1,895,016 | 165,556,364 | 27,793,561 | 1,867,810 | 168,602,602 | 28,471,058 |
| wel | 275,500 | 24,365,692 | 7,481,644 | 278,442 | 26,649,585 | 8,232,320 | 283,130 | 29,450,094 | 8,650,699 |
| Total | 27,900,545 | $2,426,754,151 | $628,343,355 | 27,966,918 | $2,604,604,322 | $666,756,260 | 28,082,931 | $2,863,085,064 | $712,405,125 |

[a] Data obtained from denominational source.

[b] YACC Church of the Brethren figures reported for 15 months due to fiscal year change; adjusted here to 12/15ths.

[c] The Presbyterian Church (USA) data for 1973 combines United Presbyterian Church in the U.S.A. data for 1973 (see YACC 1975) and an average of Presbyterian Church in the United States data for 1972 and 1974, since 1973 data was not reported in the YACC series.

Appendix B-1: Church Member Giving, 1968-1997 (continued)

| | Data Year 1974 | | | Data Year 1975 | | | Data Year 1976 | | |
|---|---|---|---|---|---|---|---|---|---|
| | Full/Confirmed Members | Congregational Finances | Benevolences | Full/Confirmed Members | Congregational Finances | Benevolences | Full/Confirmed Members | Congregational Finances | Benevolences |
| abc | 1,176,989 a | $147,022,280 | $21,847,285 | 1,180,793 a | $153,697,091 | $23,638,372 | 1,142,773 a | $163,134,092 | $25,792,357 |
| alc | 1,764,186 | 173,318,574 | 38,921,546 | 1,764,810 | 198,863,519 | 75,666,809 | 1,768,758 | 215,527,544 | 76,478,278 |
| arp | 28,570 | 3,935,533 a | 868,284 a | 28,589 | 4,820,846 a | 929,880 a | 28,581 | 5,034,270 a | 1,018,913 a |
| bcc | 10,255 | 3,002,218 | 1,078,576 | 10,784 | 3,495,152 | 955,845 | 11,375 | 4,088,492 | 1,038,484 |
| ccd | 854,844 | 119,434,435 | 20,818,434 | 859,885 | 126,553,931 | 22,126,459 | 845,058 | 135,008,269 | 23,812,274 |
| cga | 161,401 | 39,189,287 | 7,343,123 | 166,259 | 42,077,029 | 7,880,559 | 170,285 | 47,191,302 | 8,854,295 |
| cgg | 7,455 | 975,000 | 105,000 | 7,485 | 990,000 | 105,000 | 7,620 | 1,100,000 | 105,000 |
| chb | 179,387 | 18,609,614 | 7,281,551 | 179,336 | 20,338,351 | 7,842,819 | 178,157 | 22,133,858 | 8,032,293 |
| chn | 430,128 | 104,774,391 | 25,534,267 a | 441,093 | 115,400,881 | 28,186,392 a | 448,658 | 128,294,499 | 32,278,187 a |
| ccc | 21,661 a | 2,452,254 a | 1,181,655 a | 22,065 a | 2,639,472 a | 1,750,364 a | 21,703 a | 3,073,413 a | 1,494,355 a |
| cpc | 55,577 | 9,619,526 | 1,087,680 | 90,005 | 11,392,729 | 1,215,279 | 88,382 | 10,919,882 | 1,648,770 |
| ecc | 29,636 a | 4,901,100 a | 1,009,726 a | 28,886 a | 5,503,484 a | 1,068,134 a | 28,840 a | 6,006,621 a | 1,139,209 a |
| ecv | 69,960 | 21,235,204 a | 5,131,124 | 71,808 | 23,440,265 a | 6,353,422 | 73,458 | 25,686,916 a | 6,898,871 |
| elc | ALC & LCA | ALC & LCA | ALC & LCA | ALC & LCA | ALC & LCA | ALC & LCA | ALC & LCA | ALC & LCA | ALC & LCA |
| els | 13,097 | 1,519,749 | 411,732 a | 13,489 a | 1,739,255 | 438,875 a | 14,504 | 2,114,998 | 521,018 a |
| emc | 3,123 | 644,548 | 548,000 | NA | NA | NA | 3,350 | 800,000 | 628,944 |
| feb | 49,314 a | NA | NA | NA | NA | NA | NA | NA | NA |
| fmc | NA | 16,734,865 | 7,373,664 | 50,632 | 18,336,422 | 8,143,838 | 51,565 | 19,954,186 | 9,261,347 |
| fum | NA | NA | NA | 56,605 | 6,428,458 | 1,551,036 | 51,032 | 6,749,045 | 1,691,190 |
| ggb | NA | NA | NA | NA | NA | NA | NA | NA | NA |
| lca | 2,166,615 | 228,081,405 | 44,531,126 | 2,183,131 | 222,637,156 | 55,646,303 | 2,187,995 | 243,449,466 | 58,761,005 |
| lms | 2,010,456 | 249,150,470 | 55,076,955 | 2,018,530 | 266,546,758 | 55,896,061 | 2,026,336 | 287,098,403 | 56,831,860 |
| mch | 92,930 a | 13,792,266 | 9,887,051 | 94,209 | 15,332,908 | 11,860,385 | 96,092 a | 17,215,234 | 12,259,924 |
| mca | 25,583 | 3,304,388 | 513,685 | 25,512 | 3,567,406 | 552,512 | 24,938 | 4,088,195 | 573,619 |
| nab | 41,437 | 6,604,693 | 2,142,148 | 42,122 | 7,781,298 | 2,470,317 | 42,277 | 8,902,540 | 3,302,348 |
| opc | NA | NA | NA | NA | NA | NA | 10,372 | 3,287,612 | 892,889 |
| pch | 3,619,768 | 502,237,350 | 100,966,089 | 3,535,825 | 529,327,006 | 111,027,318 | 3,484,985 | 563,106,353 | 125,035,379 |
| rca | 210,866 a | 41,053,364 a | 11,470,631 a | 212,349 a | 44,681,053 a | 11,994,379 a | 211,628 a | 49,083,734 a | 13,163,739 a |
| sda | 479,799 | 67,241,956 | 166,166,766 | 495,699 | 72,060,121 | 184,689,250 | 509,792 | 81,577,130 | 184,648,454 |
| sbc | 12,513,378 | 1,123,264,849 | 219,214,770 | 12,733,124 | 1,237,594,037 | 237,452,055 | 12,917,992 | 1,382,794,494 | 262,144,889 |
| ucc | 1,841,312 | 184,292,017 | 30,243,223 | 1,818,762 | 193,524,114 | 32,125,332 | 1,801,241 | 207,486,324 | 33,862,658 |
| wel | 286,858 | 32,683,492 | 10,002,869 | 293,237 | 35,889,331 | 11,212,937 | 297,862 | 40,017,991 | 11,300,102 |
| Total | 28,144,585 | $3,114,883,698 | $790,756,960 | 28,425,024 | $3,361,093,785 | $902,779,932 | 28,545,609 | $3,680,689,491 | $963,470,651 |

aData obtained from denominational source.

# Appendix B-1: Church Member Giving, 1968-1997 (continued)

| | Data Year 1977 | | | Data Year 1978 | | | Data Year 1979 | | |
|---|---|---|---|---|---|---|---|---|---|
| | Full/Confirmed Members | Congregational Finances | Benevolences | Full/Confirmed Members | Congregational Finances | Benevolences | Full/Confirmed Members | Congregational Finances | Benevolences |
| abc | 1,146,084 a | $172,710,063 | $27,765,800 | 1,008,495 a | $184,716,172 | $31,937,862 | 1,036,054 a | $195,986,995 | $34,992,300 |
| alc | 1,772,227 | 231,960,304 | 54,085,201 | 1,773,179 | 256,371,804 | 57,145,861 | 1,768,071 | 284,019,905 | 63,903,906 |
| arp | 28,371 a | 5,705,295 a | 1,061,285 a | 28,644 | 6,209,447 a | 1,031,469 a | 28,513 | 6,544,759 a | 1,125,562 a |
| bcc | NA | NA | NA | NA | NA | NA | 12,923 | 5,519,037 | 1,312,046 |
| ccd | 817,288 | 148,880,340 | 25,698,856 | 791,633 | 166,249,455 | 25,790,367 | 773,765 | 172,270,978 | 27,335,440 |
| cga | 171,947 | 51,969,150 | 10,001,062 | 173,753 | 57,630,848 | 11,214,530 | 175,113 | 65,974,517 | 12,434,621 |
| cgg | 7,595 | 1,130,000 | 110,000 | 7,550 | 1,135,000 | 110,000 | 7,620 | 1,170,000 | 105,000 |
| chb | 177,534 | 23,722,817 | 8,228,903 | 175,335 | 25,397,531 | 9,476,220 | 172,115 | 28,422,684 | 10,161,266 |
| chn | 455,100 | 141,807,024 | 34,895,751 a | 462,124 | 153,943,138 | 38,300,431 a | 473,726 | 170,515,940 a | 42,087,862 a |
| ccc | 21,897 a | 3,916,248 a | 1,554,143 a | 22,364 a | 4,271,435 a | 1,630,565 a | 23,481 a | 4,969,610 a | 1,871,754 a |
| cpc | 88,353 | 11,611,365 | 1,781,862 | 88,093 | 13,657,931 | 2,136,706 | 89,218 | 13,905,745 | 2,513,625 |
| ecc | 28,712 a | 6,356,730 a | 1,271,310 a | 28,459 a | 6,890,381 a | 1,454,826 a | 27,995 a | 7,552,495 a | 1,547,857 a |
| ecv | 74,060 | 28,758,357 a | 7,240,548 | 74,678 | 32,606,550 a | 8,017,623 | 76,092 | 37,118,906 a | 9,400,074 |
| elc | ALC & LCA | ALC & LCA | ALC & LCA | ALC & LCA | ALC & LCA | ALC & LCA | ALC & LCA | ALC & LCA | ALC & LCA |
| els | 14,652 | 2,290,697 | 546,899 a | 14,833 | 2,629,719 | 833,543 a | 15,081 | 2,750,703 | 904,774 a |
| emc | NA | NA | NA | 3,634 | 1,281,761 | 794,896 | 3,704 | 1,380,806 | 828,264 |
| feb | NA | NA | NA | 3,956 | 970,960 | 745,059 | NA | NA | NA |
| fmc | 52,563 | 22,417,964 | 10,163,648 | 55,493 | 23,911,458 | 10,121,800 | NA | NA | NA |
| fum | 52,599 | 6,943,990 | 1,895,984 | 53,390 | 8,172,337 | 1,968,884 | 51,426 | 6,662,787 | 2,131,108 |
| ggb | 72,030 | 9,854,533 | 747,842 | NA | NA | NA | 73,046 | 13,131,345 | 1,218,763 |
| lca | 2,191,942 | 251,083,883 | 62,076,894 | 2,183,666 | 277,186,563 | 72,426,148 | 2,177,231 | 301,605,382 | 71,325,097 |
| lms | 1,991,408 | 301,064,630 | 57,077,162 | 1,969,279 | 329,134,237 | 59,030,753 | 1,965,422 | 360,989,735 | 63,530,596 |
| mch | 96,609 | 18,540,237 | 12,980,502 | 97,142 | 22,922,417 | 14,124,757 a | 98,027 | 24,505,346 | 15,116,762 |
| mca | 25,323 | 4,583,616 | 581,200 | 24,854 | 4,441,750 | 625,536 | 24,782 | 4,600,331 | 689,070 |
| nab | 42,724 | 10,332,556 | 3,554,204 | 42,499 | 11,629,309 | 3,559,983 | 42,779 | 13,415,024 | 3,564,339 |
| opc | 10,920 | 3,514,172 | 931,935 | 10,939 | 4,107,705 | 1,135,388 | 11,300 | 4,683,302 | 1,147,191 |
| pch | 3,430,927 | 633,187,916 | 130,252,348 | 3,382,783 | 692,872,811 | 128,194,954 | 3,321,787 | 776,049,247 | 148,528,993 |
| rca | 210,637 a | 53,999,791 a | 14,210,966 a | 211,778 a | 60,138,720 a | 15,494,816 a | 210,700 a | 62,997,526 a | 16,750,408 a |
| sda | 522,317 | 98,468,365 | 216,202,975 | 535,705 | 104,044,989 | 226,692,736 | 553,089 | 118,711,906 | 255,936,372 |
| sbc | 13,078,239 | 1,506,877,921 | 289,179,711 | 13,191,394 | 1,668,120,760 | 316,462,385 | 13,372,757 | 1,864,213,869 | 355,885,769 |
| ucc | 1,785,652 | 219,878,772 | 35,522,221 | 1,769,104 | 232,593,033 | 37,789,958 | 1,745,533 | 249,443,032 | 41,100,583 |
| wel | 301,944 | 44,492,259 | 11,639,834 | 303,944 | 50,255,539 | 12,960,885 | 306,264 | 54,983,467 | 14,230,208 |
| Total | 28,669,654 | $4,010,831,814 | $1,021,259,046 | 28,488,700 | $4,397,087,918 | $1,091,208,941 | 28,637,614 | $4,846,963,757 | $1,201,679,610 |

[a]Data obtained from denominational source.

## Appendix B-1: Church Member Giving, 1968-1997 (continued)

| | Data Year 1980 | | | Data Year 1981 | | | Data Year 1982 | | |
|---|---|---|---|---|---|---|---|---|---|
| | Full/Confirmed Members | Congregational Finances | Benevolences | Full/Confirmed Members | Congregational Finances | Benevolences | Full/Confirmed Members | Congregational Finances | Benevolences |
| abc | 1,008,700 a | $213,560,656 | $37,133,159 | 989,322 a | $227,931,461 | $40,046,261 | 983,580 a | $242,750,027 | $41,457,745 |
| alc | 1,763,067 | 312,592,610 | 65,235,739 | 1,758,452 | 330,155,588 | 96,102,638 | 1,758,239 | 359,848,865 | 77,010,444 |
| arp | 28,166 a | 6,868,650 a | 1,054,229 a | 28,334 a | 7,863,221 a | 1,497,838 a | 29,087 a | 8,580,311 a | 1,807,572 a |
| bcc | NA | NA | NA | 13,993 | 6,781,857 | 1,740,711 | NA | NA | NA |
| ccd | 788,394 | 189,176,399 | 30,991,519 | 772,466 | 211,828,751 | 31,067,142 | 770,227 | 227,178,861 | 34,307,638 |
| cga | 176,429 | 67,367,485 | 13,414,112 | 178,581 | 78,322,907 | 14,907,277 | 184,685 | 84,896,806 | 17,171,600 |
| cgg | NA | NA | NA | 5,981 | 1,788,298 | 403,000 | NA | NA | NA |
| chb | 170,839 | 29,813,265 | 11,663,976 | 170,267 | 31,641,019 | 12,929,076 | 168,844 | 35,064,568 | 12,844,415 |
| chn | 483,101 | 191,536,556 | 45,786,446 a | 490,852 | 203,145,992 | 50,084,163 a | 497,261 | 221,947,940 | 53,232,461 a |
| ccc | 24,410 a | 6,017,539 a | 2,169,298 a | 25,044 a | 8,465,804 | 2,415,233 | 26,008 | 9,230,111 | 2,574,569 |
| cpc | 90,844 | 16,448,164 | 2,835,695 | 91,665 | 17,225,308 | 3,504,763 | 91,774 | 18,600,022 | 2,703,521 |
| ecc | 27,567 a | 8,037,564 a | 1,630,993 a | 27,287 a | 8,573,057 a | 1,758,025 a | 27,203 a | 9,119,278 a | 1,891,936 a |
| ecv | 77,737 | 41,888,556 a | 10,031,072 | 79,523 | 45,206,565 a | 8,689,918 | 81,324 | 50,209,520 a | 8,830,793 |
| elc | ALC & LCA | ALC & LCA | ALC & LCA | ALC & LCA | ALC & LCA | ALC & LCA | ALC & LCA | ALC & LCA | ALC & LCA |
| els | 14,968 | 3,154,804 | 876,929 a | 14,904 | 3,461,387 | 716,624 | 15,165 | 3,767,977 | 804,822 |
| emc | 3,782 | 1,527,945 | 1,041,447 | 3,753 | 1,515,975 | 908,342 | 3,832 | 1,985,890 | 731,510 |
| feb | 4,329 | 1,250,466 | 627,536 | NA | NA | NA | 2,047 | 696,660 | 1,020,972 |
| fmc | NA | NA | NA | NA | NA | NA | 54,198 | 35,056,434 | 8,051,593 |
| fum | 51,691 | 9,437,724 | 2,328,137 | 51,248 | 9,551,765 | 2,449,731 | 50,601 | 10,334,180 | 2,597,215 |
| ggb | 74,159 | 14,967,312 | 1,547,038 | 75,028 | 15,816,060 | 1,473,070 | NA | NA | NA |
| lca | 2,176,991 | 371,981,816 | 87,439,137 | 2,173,558 | 404,300,509 | 82,862,299 | 2,176,265 | 435,564,519 | 83,217,264 |
| lms | 1,973,958 | 390,756,268 | 66,626,364 | 1,983,198 | 429,910,406 | 86,341,102 | 1,961,260 | 468,468,156 | 75,457,846 |
| mch | 99,511 | 28,846,931 | 16,437,738 | 99,651 | 31,304,278 | 17,448,024 | 101,501 | 33,583,338 | 17,981,274 |
| mca | 24,863 | 5,178,444 | 860,399 | 24,500 | 5,675,495 | 831,177 | 24,669 | 6,049,857 | 812,015 |
| nab | 43,041 | 12,453,858 | 3,972,485 | 43,146 | 15,513,286 | 4,420,403 | 42,735 | 17,302,952 | 4,597,515 |
| opc | 11,550 | 5,235,294 | 1,235,849 | 11,889 | 5,939,983 | 1,382,451 | NA | NA | NA |
| pch | 3,262,086 | 820,218,732 | 176,172,729 | 3,202,392 | 896,641,430 | 188,576,382 | 3,157,372 | 970,223,947 | 199,331,832 |
| rca | 210,762 | 70,733,297 | 17,313,239 a | 210,312 | 77,044,709 | 18,193,793 a | 211,168 | 82,656,050 | 19,418,165 a |
| sda | 571,141 | 121,484,768 | 275,783,385 | 588,536 | 133,088,131 | 297,838,046 | 606,310 | 136,877,455 | 299,437,917 |
| sbc | 13,600,126 | 2,080,375,258 | 400,976,072 | 13,782,644 | 2,336,062,506 | 443,931,179 | 13,991,709 | 2,628,272,553 | 486,402,607 |
| ucc | 1,736,244 | 278,546,571 | 44,042,186 | 1,726,535 | 300,730,591 | 48,329,399 | 1,708,847 | 323,725,191 | 52,738,069 |
| wel | 308,620 | 60,624,862 | 16,037,844 | 311,351 | 68,056,396 | 18,261,099 | 312,195 | 71,891,457 a | 18,677,343 |
| Total | 28,807,076 | $5,351,384,560 | $1,335,264,752 | 28,934,412 | $5,906,220,962 | $1,479,109,166 | 29,038,106 | $6,486,273,014 | $1,525,110,653 |

[a] Data obtained from denominational source.

96

## Appendix B-1: Church Member Giving, 1968-1997 (continued)

| | Data Year 1983 | | | Data Year 1984 | | | Data Year 1985 | | |
|---|---|---|---|---|---|---|---|---|---|
| | Full/Confirmed Members | Congregational Finances | Benevolences | Full/Confirmed Members | Congregational Finances | Benevolences | Full/Confirmed Members | Congregational Finances | Benevolences |
| abc | 965,117 a | $254,716,036 | $43,683,021 | 953,945 a | $267,556,088 | $46,232,040 | 894,732 a | $267,694,684 | $47,201,119 |
| alc | 1,756,420 | 375,500,188 | 84,633,617 | 1,756,558 | 413,876,101 | 86,601,067 | 1,751,649 | 428,861,660 | 87,152,699 |
| arp | 31,738 | 10,640,050 a | 2,180,230 a | 31,355 | 11,221,526 a | 3,019,456 a | 32,051 | 12,092,868 a | 3,106,994 a |
| bcc | 14,782 | 7,638,413 | 1,858,632 | 15,128 | 8,160,359 | 2,586,843 | 15,535 a | 8,504,354 a | 2,979,046 a |
| ccd | 761,629 | 241,934,972 | 35,809,331 | 755,233 | 263,694,210 | 38,402,791 | 743,486 | 274,072,301 | 40,992,053 |
| cga | 182,190 | 81,309,323 | 13,896,753 | 185,404 | 86,611,269 | 14,347,570 | 185,593 | 91,078,512 | 15,308,954 |
| cgg | 5,759 | 1,981,300 | 412,000 | 4,711 | 2,211,800 | 504,200 | 4,575 | 2,428,730 | 582,411 |
| chb | 164,680 | 39,726,743 | 14,488,192 | 161,824 | 37,743,527 | 15,136,600 | 159,184 | 40,658,904 | 16,509,718 |
| chn | 506,439 | 237,220,642 | 57,267,073 a | 514,937 | 253,566,280 | 60,909,810 a | 520,741 | 267,134,078 | 65,627,515 a |
| ccc | 26,691 a | 9,189,221 a | 2,980,636 | 28,383 | 10,018,982 | 3,051,425 | 28,624 | 11,729,365 | 3,350,021 |
| cpc | 93,387 | 20,206,646 | 2,604,569 | 92,242 | 21,185,481 | 3,843,056 | 85,346 a | 21,241,302 a | 3,227,932 a |
| ecc | 26,769 a | 9,505,479 a | 2,019,373 a | 26,375 a | 10,302,554 a | 2,220,852 a | 26,016 | 8,134,641 a | 1,777,172 |
| ecv | 82,943 | 53,279,350 a | 10,615,909 | 84,185 | 60,295,634 a | 11,243,908 | 85,150 | 63,590,735 a | 13,828,030 |
| elc | ALC & LCA | ALC & LCA | ALC & LCA | ALC & LCA | ALC & LCA | ALC & LCA | ALC & LCA | ALC & LCA | ALC & LCA |
| els | 15,576 | 3,842,625 | 838,788 | 15,396 | 4,647,714 | 931,677 a | 15,012 | 4,725,783 | 791,586 |
| emc | 3,857 | 1,930,689 | 738,194 | 3,908 | 2,017,565 | 862,350 | 3,813 | 2,128,019 | 1,058,040 |
| feb | 2,094 | 622,467 | 1,466,399 | NA | NA | NA | 2,107 a | 1,069,851 a | 402,611 a |
| fmc | NA | NA | NA | NA | NA | NA | 56,242 | 42,046,626 a | 9,461,369 a |
| fum | 49,441 | 11,723,240 | 2,886,931 | 48,713 | 11,549,163 | 2,875,370 | 48,812 | 12,601,820 | 3,012,658 |
| ggb | 75,133 | 17,283,259 | 1,733,755 | 75,028 | 17,599,169 | 1,729,228 | 73,040 | 18,516,252 | 1,683,130 |
| lca | 2,176,772 | 457,239,780 | 88,909,363 | 2,168,594 | 496,228,216 | 99,833,067 | 2,161,216 | 539,142,069 | 103,534,375 |
| lms | 1,984,199 | 499,220,552 | 76,991,991 a | 1,986,392 | 539,346,935 | 81,742,006 a | 1,982,753 | 566,507,516 | 83,117,911 a |
| mch | 103,350 a | 34,153,628 | 17,581,878 | 90,347 | 37,333,306 | 16,944,094 | 91,167 | 34,015,200 | 25,593,500 |
| mca | 24,913 | 6,618,339 | 911,787 | 24,269 | 7,723,611 | 1,183,741 | 24,396 | 8,698,949 | 1,170,349 |
| nab | 43,286 | 18,010,853 | 5,132,672 | 43,215 | 19,322,720 | 5,724,552 | 42,863 | 20,246,236 | 5,766,686 |
| opc | 12,045 | 6,874,722 | 1,755,169 | 12,239 | 7,555,006 | 2,079,924 | 12,634 | 8,291,483 | 2,204,998 |
| pch | 3,122,213 | 1,047,756,995 | 197,981,080 | 3,092,151 | 1,132,098,779 | 218,412,639 | 3,057,226 a | 1,252,885,684 a | 232,487,569 a |
| rca | 211,660 | 92,071,986 | 20,632,574 | 209,968 a | 100,378,778 | 21,794,880 | 209,395 | 103,428,950 | 22,233,299 |
| sda | 623,563 | 143,636,140 | 323,461,439 | 638,929 | 155,257,063 | 319,664,449 | 651,594 | 155,077,180 | 346,251,406 |
| sbc | 14,178,051 | 2,838,573,815 | 528,781,000 | 14,341,822 | 3,094,913,877 | 567,467,188 | 14,477,364 | 3,272,276,486 | 609,868,694 |
| ucc | 1,701,513 | 332,613,396 | 55,716,557 | 1,696,107 | 385,786,198 | 58,679,094 | 1,683,777 | 409,543,989 | 62,169,679 a |
| wel | 313,883 | 76,133,614 a | 24,169,441 | 315,466 | 82,884,471 a | 22,951,699 | 316,297 a | 87,194,889 a | 22,376,423 a |
| Total | 29,260,093 | $6,924,272,847 | $1,642,439,413 | 29,372,824 | $7,532,404,141 | $1,733,627,368 | 29,442,390 | $8,026,747,690 | $1,856,901,159 |

aData obtained from denominational source.

## Appendix B-1: Church Member Giving, 1968-1997 (continued)

| | Data Year 1986 | | | Data Year 1987 | | | Data Year 1988 | | |
|---|---|---|---|---|---|---|---|---|---|
| | Full/Confirmed Members | Congregational Finances | Benevolences | Full/Confirmed Members | Congregational Finances | Benevolences | Full/Confirmed Members | Congregational Finances | Benevolences |
| abc | 862,582 a | $287,020,378 a | $49,070,083 a | 868,189 a | $291,606,418 a | $55,613,855 | 825,102 a | $296,569,316 a | $55,876,771 |
| alc | 1,740,439 | 434,641,736 | 96,147,129 | See ELCA | See ELCA | See ELCA | See ELCA | See ELCA | See ELCA |
| arp | 32,438 a | 12,336,321 a | 3,434,408 a | 32,289 | 13,553,176 a | 3,927,030 a | 31,922 | 13,657,776 a | 5,063,036 a |
| bcc | 15,911 | 10,533,883 | 2,463,558 | 16,136 | 11,203,321 | 3,139,949 | NA | NA | NA |
| ccd | 732,466 | 288,277,386 | 42,027,504 | 718,522 | 287,464,332 | 42,728,826 | 707,985 | 297,187,996 | 42,226,128 |
| cga | 188,662 | 91,768,855 | 16,136,647 | 198,552 | 124,376,413 | 20,261,687 | 198,842 | 132,384,232 | 19,781,941 |
| cgg | NA | NA | NA | 4,348 | 2,437,778 | 738,818 | NA | NA | NA |
| chb | 155,967 | 43,531,293 | 17,859,101 | 154,067 | 45,201,732 | 19,342,402 | 151,169 | 48,008,657 | 19,701,942 a |
| chn | 529,192 | 283,189,977 | 68,438,998 a | 541,878 | 294,160,356 | 73,033,568 a | 550,700 | 309,478,442 | 74,737,057 a |
| ccc | 28,948 | 15,559,846 a | 3,961,037 | 29,429 | 15,409,349 a | 3,740,688 | 29,015 | 13,853,547 | 4,120,974 |
| cpc | 91,556 | 22,992,625 | 3,782,282 | 85,781 | 22,857,711 | 3,727,681 | 85,304 | 23,366,911 d | 3,722,607 |
| ecc | 25,625 | 10,977,813 a | 2,422,879 a | 25,300 | 14,281,140 a | 2,575,415 a | 24,980 | 12,115,762 | 2,856,766 a |
| ecv | 86,079 | 67,889,353 a | 14,374,707 | 86,741 | 73,498,123 a | 14,636,000 | 87,750 | 77,504,445 a | 14,471,178 |
| elc | ALC & LCA | ALC & LCA | ALC & LCA | 3,952,663 | 1,083,293,684 | 169,685,942 | 3,931,878 | 1,150,483,034 | 169,580,472 |
| els | 15,083 a | 4,996,111 a | 1,050,715 a | 15,892 | 5,298,882 | 1,082,198 | NA | NA | NA |
| emc | NA | NA | NA | 3,841 | 2,332,216 | 1,326,711 | 3,879 | 2,522,533 | 1,438,459 |
| feb | NA | NA | NA | NA | NA | NA | NA | NA | NA |
| fmc | 56,243 | 46,150,881 | 9,446,120 | 57,262 | 47,743,298 | 9,938,096 | 57,432 | 48,788,041 | 9,952,103 |
| fum | 48,143 | 12,790,909 | 2,916,870 | 47,173 | 13,768,272 | 3,631,353 | 48,325 | 14,127,491 | 3,719,125 |
| ggb | 72,263 | 19,743,265 | 1,883,826 | 73,515 | 20,850,827 | 1,789,578 | 74,086 | 21,218,051 | 1,731,299 |
| lca | 2,157,701 | 569,250,519 | 111,871,174 | See ELCA | See ELCA | See ELCA | See ELCA | See ELCA | See ELCA |
| lms | 1,974,798 | 605,768,688 | 87,803,646 a | 1,973,347 | 620,271,274 | 86,938,723 a | 1,962,674 | 659,288,332 | 88,587,175 a |
| mch | 91,467 a | 40,097,500 a | 24,404,200 a | 92,673 a | 43,295,100 | 25,033,600 | 92,682 | 47,771,200 | 27,043,900 |
| mca | 24,260 | 8,133,127 | 1,155,350 | 24,440 | 9,590,658 | 1,174,593 | 23,526 | 9,221,646 | 1,210,476 |
| nab | 42,084 | 20,961,799 | 5,982,391 | NA | NA | NA | 42,629 | 24,597,288 | 6,611,840 |
| opc | NA | NA | NA | 13,301 | 9,884,288 | 2,425,480 | NA | NA | NA |
| pch | 3,007,322 | 1,318,440,264 | 249,033,881 | 2,967,781 | 1,395,501,073 | 247,234,439 | 2,929,608 | 1,439,655,217 | 284,989,138 |
| rca | 207,993 | 114,231,429 | 22,954,596 | 203,581 | 114,652,192 a | 24,043,270 | 200,631 | 127,409,263 | 25,496,802 a |
| sda | 666,199 | 166,692,974 | 361,316,753 | 675,702 | 166,939,355 | 374,830,065 | 687,200 | 178,768,967 | 395,849,223 |
| sbc | 14,613,638 | 3,481,124,471 | 635,196,984 | 14,722,617 | 3,629,842,643 | 662,455,177 | 14,812,844 | 3,706,652,161 | 689,366,904 |
| ucc | 1,676,105 | 429,340,239 | 63,808,091 | 1,662,568 | 451,700,210 | 66,870,922 | 1,644,787 | 470,747,740 | 65,734,348 |
| wel | 316,416 | 92,662,969 a | 22,448,920 | 317,294 | 97,567,101 a | 22,207,123 | 316,987 | 101,975,092 a | 22,406,238 |
| Total | 29,459,580 | $8,488,843,830 | $1,945,526,401 | 29,564,882 | $8,908,580,922 | $1,966,875,491 | 29,521,937 | $9,227,353,140 | $2,060,383,568 |

a Data obtained from denominational source.
d A YACC prepublication data table listed 23,366,911 for Congregational Finances which, added to Benevolences, equals the published Total of 27,089,518.

# Appendix B-1: Church Member Giving, 1968-1997 (continued)

| | Data Year 1989 | | | Data Year 1990 | | | Data Year 1991 | | |
|---|---|---|---|---|---|---|---|---|---|
| | Full/Confirmed Members | Congregational Finances | Benevolences | Full/Confirmed Members | Congregational Finances | Benevolences | Full/Confirmed Members | Congregational Finances | Benevolences |
| abc | 789,730 a | $305,212,094 a | $55,951,539 | 764,890 a | $315,777,005 a | $54,740,278 | 773,838 a | $318,150,548 a | $52,330,924 a |
| alc | See ELCA | See ELCA | See ELCA | See ELCA | See ELCA | See ELCA | See ELCA | See ELCA | See ELCA |
| arp | 32,600 | 16,053,762 a | 4,367,314 a | 32,817 a | 17,313,355 a | 5,031,504 a | 33,494 a | 17,585,273 a | 5,254,738 a |
| bcc | 16,842 | 12,840,038 | 3,370,306 | 17,277 | 13,327,414 | 3,336,580 | 17,456 a | 14,491,918 a | 3,294,169 a |
| ccd | 690,115 | 310,043,826 | 42,015,246 | 678,750 | 321,569,909 | 42,607,007 | 663,336 | 331,629,009 | 43,339,307 |
| cga | 199,786 | 134,918,052 | 20,215,075 | 205,884 | 141,375,027 | 21,087,504 | 214,743 a | 146,249,447 a | 21,801,570 a |
| cgg | 4,415 | 3,367,000 | 686,000 | 4,399 | 3,106,729 | 690,000 | 4,375 | 2,756,651 | 662,500 |
| chb | 149,681 | 51,921,820 | 19,737,714 a | 148,253 | 54,832,226 | 18,384,483 a | 147,954 a | 55,035,355 a | 19,694,919 a |
| chn | 558,664 | 322,924,598 | 76,625,913 a | 563,756 a | 333,397,255 a | 77,991,665 a | 572,153 | 352,654,251 | 82,276,097 a |
| ccc | 28,413 | 18,199,823 | 4,064,111 | 28,355 | 16,964,128 | 4,174,133 | 28,035 | 17,760,290 | 4,304,052 |
| cpc | 84,866 | 25,326,430 | 4,092,869 | 91,857 | 28,364,344 | 4,355,823 | 91,650 a | 29,442,581 a | 5,972,155 a |
| ecc | 24,606 | 13,274,756 a | 2,703,095 a | 24,437 | 12,947,150 a | 2,858,077 a | 24,124 a | 13,100,036 a | 3,074,660 a |
| ecv | 89,014 | 80,621,293 a | 15,206,265 | 89,735 | 84,263,236 a | 15,601,475 | 89,648 | 87,321,563 a | 16,598,656 |
| elc | 3,909,302 | 1,239,433,257 | 182,386,940 | 3,898,478 | 1,318,884,279 | 184,174,554 | 3,890,947 | 1,375,439,787 | 186,016,168 |
| els | 15,740 | 6,186,648 | 1,342,321 | 16,181 | 6,527,076 | 1,193,789 | 16,004 | 6,657,338 | 1,030,445 |
| emc | 3,888 | 2,712,843 | 1,567,728 | 4,026 | 2,991,485 | 1,800,593 | 3,958 | 3,394,563 | 1,790,115 |
| feb | NA | NA | NA | NA | NA | NA | 2,008 a | 1,398,968 a | 500,092 a |
| fmc | 59,418 a | 50,114,090 a | 10,311,535 a | 58,084 | 55,229,181 | 10,118,505 | 57,794 | 57,880,464 | 9,876,739 |
| fum | 47,228 | 16,288,644 | 4,055,624 | 45,691 | 10,036,083 | 2,511,063 | 50,803 e | NA | NA |
| ggb | 73,738 | 23,127,835 | 1,768,804 | 74,156 | 23,127,835 | 1,737,011 | 71,119 a | 22,362,874 a | 1,408,262 a |
| lca | See ELCA | See ELCA | See ELCA | See ELCA | See ELCA | See ELCA | See ELCA | See ELCA | See ELCA |
| lms | 1,961,114 | 701,701,168 a | 90,974,340 a | 1,954,350 | 712,235,204 | 96,308,765 a | 1,952,845 | 741,823,412 | 94,094,637 a |
| mch | 92,517 | 55,353,313 | 27,873,241 | 92,448 a | 65,709,827 | 28,397,083 | 93,114 a | 68,926,324 | 28,464,199 |
| mca | 23,802 | 10,415,640 | 1,284,233 | 23,526 | 10,105,037 | 1,337,616 | 22,887 | 10,095,337 | 1,205,335 |
| nab | 42,629 | 28,076,077 | 3,890,017 | 44,493 | 31,103,672 | 7,700,119 | 43,187 a | 27,335,239 a | 7,792,876 a |
| opc | NA | NA | NA | NA | NA | NA | 12,265 | 11,700,000 | 2,700,000 |
| pch | 2,886,482 | 1,528,450,805 | 295,365,032 | 2,847,437 | 1,530,341,707 | 294,990,441 | 2,805,548 | 1,636,407,042 | 311,905,934 a |
| rca | 198,832 | 136,796,188 a | 29,456,132 a | 197,154 | 144,357,953 a | 27,705,029 a | 193,531 a | 147,532,382 a | 26,821,721 a |
| sda | 701,781 | 196,204,538 | 415,752,350 | 717,446 | 195,054,218 | 433,035,080 | 733,026 | 201,411,183 | 456,242,995 |
| sbc | 14,907,826 | 3,873,300,782 | 712,738,838 | 15,038,409 | 4,146,285,561 | 718,174,874 | 15,232,347 | 4,283,283,059 | 731,812,766 |
| ucc | 1,625,969 | 496,825,160 | 72,300,698 | 1,599,212 | 527,378,397 | 71,984,897 | 1,583,830 | 543,803,752 | 73,149,887 |
| wel | 317,117 | 110,575,539 a | 22,811,571 | 316,813 | 116,272,092 a | 24,088,568 | 316,929 a | 121,835,547 a | 24,276,370 a |
| Total | 29,536,115 | $9,770,266,019 | $2,150,452,093 | 29,578,314 | $10,238,877,385 | $2,189,036,831 | 29,692,145 | $10,647,464,193 | $2,248,530,078 |

[a] Data obtained from denominational source.
[e] Inclusive membership, used only in Chapter 5 analysis.

# Appendix B-1: Church Member Giving, 1968-1997 (continued)

| | Data Year 1992 | | | Data Year 1993 | | | Data Year 1994 | | |
|---|---|---|---|---|---|---|---|---|---|
| | Full/Confirmed Members | Congregational Finances | Benevolences | Full/Confirmed Members | Congregational Finances | Benevolences | Full/Confirmed Members | Congregational Finances | Benevolences |
| abc | 730,009 a | $310,307,040 a | $52,764,005 | 764,657 a | $346,658,047 a | $53,562,811 | 697,379 a | $337,185,885 a | $51,553,256 a |
| alc | See ELCA | See ELCA | See ELCA | See ELCA | See ELCA | See ELCA | See ELCA | See ELCA | See ELCA |
| arp | 33,550 | 18,175,957 a | 5,684,008 a | 33,662 a | 20,212,390 a | 5,822,845 a | 33,636 | 22,618,802 a | 6,727,857 |
| bcc | 17,646 a | 15,981,118 a | 3,159,717 a | 17,986 | 13,786,394 | 4,515,730 a | 18,152 | 14,844,672 | 5,622,005 |
| ccd | 655,652 | 333,629,412 | 46,440,333 | 619,028 | 328,219,027 | 44,790,415 | 605,996 | 342,352,080 | 43,165,285 |
| cga | 214,743 | 150,115,497 | 23,500,213 | 216,117 | 158,454,703 | 23,620,177 | 221,346 a | 160,694,760 a | 26,262,049 a |
| cgg | 4,085 | 2,648,085 | 509,398 | 4,239 | 2,793,000 | 587,705 | 3,996 | 2,934,843 | 475,799 |
| chb | 147,912 | 57,954,895 | 21,748,320 | 146,713 | 56,818,998 | 23,278,848 | 144,282 | 57,210,682 | 24,155,595 |
| chn | 582,804 a | 361,555,793 a | 84,118,580 a | 589,398 | 369,896,767 | 87,416,378 a | 595,303 | 387,385,034 | 89,721,860 |
| ccc | 30,387 | 22,979,946 | 4,311,234 | 36,864 | 24,997,736 a | 5,272,184 | 37,996 a | 23,758,101 a | 5,240,805 a |
| cpc | 92,240 | 29,721,914 | 4,588,604 | 91,489 | 29,430,921 | 4,852,663 | 90,125 | 31,732,121 | 4,864,472 |
| ecc | 24,150 | 13,451,827 a | 3,120,351 a | 23,889 | 13,546,159 a | 3,258,595 a | 23,504 | 13,931,409 | 3,269,986 |
| ecv | 90,985 a | 93,071,869 a | 16,732,701 a | 89,511 | 93,765,006 a | 16,482,315 | 90,919 a | 101,746,341 a | 17,874,955 a |
| elc | 3,878,055 | 1,399,419,800 | 189,605,837 | 3,861,418 | 1,452,000,815 | 188,393,158 | 3,849,692 | 1,502,746,601 | 187,145,886 |
| els | 15,929 a | 6,944,522 a | 1,271,058 a | 15,780 | 6,759,222 a | 1,100,660 | 15,960 | 7,288,521 | 1,195,698 |
| emc | 4,059 | 3,834,001 | 2,299,864 | 4,130 a | 4,260,307 a | 1,406,682 a | 4,225 a | 4,597,730 a | 1,533,157 a |
| feb | 1,872 a | 1,343,225 a | 397,553 a | 1,866 a | 1,294,646 a | 429,023 a | 1,898 a | 1,537,041 a | 395,719 a |
| fmc | 58,220 | 60,584,079 | 10,591,064 | 59,156 | 62,478,294 | 10,513,187 | 59,354 a | 65,359,325 a | 10,708,854 a |
| fum | 50,005 e | NA | NA | 45,542 e | NA | NA | 44,771 e | NA | NA |
| ggb | 72,388 a | 21,561,432 a | 1,402,330 a | 73,129 a | 22,376,970 a | 1,440,342 a | 71,140 a | 19,651,624 a | 2,052,409 a |
| lca | See ELCA | See ELCA | See ELCA | See ELCA | See ELCA | See ELCA | See ELCA | See ELCA | See ELCA |
| lms | 1,953,248 | 777,467,488 | 97,275,934 a | 1,945,077 | 789,821,559 | 96,355,945 | 1,944,905 | 817,412,113 | 96,048,560 a |
| mch | 94,222 a | 68,118,222 | 28,835,719 | 95,634 | 71,385,271 | 27,973,380 | 87,911 a | 64,651,639 | 24,830,192 |
| mca | 22,533 | 10,150,953 | 1,208,372 | 22,223 | 9,675,502 | 1,191,131 | 21,448 | 9,753,010 | 1,182,778 |
| nab | 43,446 | 28,375,947 | 7,327,594 | 43,045 | 30,676,902 | 7,454,087 | 43,236 | 32,800,560 | 7,515,707 |
| opc | 12,580 a | 12,466,266 a | 3,025,824 a | 12,924 a | 13,158,089 a | 3,039,676 a | 13,970 | 14,393,880 | 3,120,454 |
| pch | 2,780,406 | 1,696,092,968 | 309,069,530 | 2,742,192 | 1,700,918,712 | 310,375,024 | 2,698,262 | 1,800,008,292 | 307,158,749 |
| rca | 190,322 a | 147,181,320 a | 28,457,900 a | 188,551 a | 159,715,941 a | 26,009,853 a | 185,242 | 153,107,408 | 27,906,830 |
| sda | 748,687 | 191,362,737 | 476,902,779 | 761,703 | 209,524,570 | 473,769,831 | 775,349 | 229,596,444 | 503,347,816 |
| sbc | 15,358,866 | 4,462,915,112 | 751,366,698 | 15,398,642 | 4,621,157,751 | 761,298,249 | 15,614,060 | 5,263,421,764 | 815,360,696 |
| ucc | 1,555,382 | 521,190,413 | 73,906,372 | 1,530,178 | 550,847,702 | 71,046,517 | 1,501,310 | 556,540,722 | 67,269,762 |
| wel | 316,183 a | 127,858,970 a | 26,426,128 a | 315,871 | 137,187,582 | 24,587,988 | 315,302 | 142,851,919 | 23,998,935 |
| Total | 29,730,561 | $10,946,460,808 | $2,310,456,991 | 29,705,072 | $11,301,818,983 | $2,314,251,242 | 29,765,898 | $12,182,113,323 | $2,393,182,924 |

a Data obtained from denominational source.
e Inclusive membership, used only in Chapter 5 analysis.

# Appendix B-1: Church Member Giving, 1968-1997 (continued)

| | Data Year 1995 | | | Data Year 1996 | | | Data Year 1997 | | |
|---|---|---|---|---|---|---|---|---|---|
| | Full/Confirmed Members | Congregational Finances | Benevolences | Full/Confirmed Members | Congregational Finances | Benevolences | Full/Confirmed Members | Congregational Finances | Benevolences |
| abc | 726,452 a | $365,873,197 a | $57,052,333 a | 670,363 a | $351,362,401 | $55,982,392 a | 658,731 a | $312,860,507 a | $54,236,977 a |
| alc | See ELCA | See ELCA | See ELCA | See ELCA | See ELCA | See ELCA | See ELCA | See ELCA | See ELCA |
| arp | 33,513 | 23,399,372 a | 5,711,882 a | 34,117 | 24,452,824 | 5,871,337 | 34,344 | 25,241,384 a | 6,606,829 a |
| bcc | 18,529 | 16,032,149 | 5,480,828 | 18,424 | 16,892,154 | 4,748,871 | 19,016 | 17,456,379 | 5,934,414 |
| ccd | 601,237 | 357,895,652 | 42,887,958 | 586,131 | 370,210,746 | 42,877,144 | 568,921 | 381,463,761 | 43,009,412 |
| cga | 224,061 | 160,897,147 | 26,192,559 | 229,240 | 180,581,111 | 26,983,385 | 229,302 | 194,438,623 | 29,054,047 |
| cgg | 3,877 | 2,722,766 | 486,661 | 3,920 | 2,926,516 | 491,348 | 3,877 | 2,987,337 | 515,247 |
| chb | 143,121 | 60,242,418 | 22,599,214 | NA | NA | NA | NA | NA | NA |
| chn | 598,946 | 396,698,137 | 93,440,095 | 608,008 a | 419,450,850 a | 95,358,352 a | 615,632 | 433,821,462 | 99,075,440 |
| ccc | 38,853 a | 24,250,819 a | 5,483,659 a | 38,469 a | 25,834,363 a | 4,989,062 a | 38,956 | 28,204,355 | 5,167,644 |
| cpc | 87,896 | 33,535,975 | 5,051,095 | 88,066 | 34,921,064 | 5,487,460 | 88,068 | 34,375,614 | 5,585,350 |
| ecc | 23,422 | 14,830,454 | 3,301,060 | 23,091 | 14,692,608 | 3,273,685 | 22,957 | 15,658,454 | 3,460,999 |
| ecv | 91,458 | 109,776,363 a | 17,565,085 a | 91,823 a | 115,693,329 a | 18,726,756 a | 93,414 | 127,642,950 | 20,462,435 |
| elc | 3,845,063 | 1,551,842,465 | 188,107,066 | 3,838,750 | 1,629,909,672 | 191,476,141 | 3,844,169 | 1,731,806,133 | 201,115,441 |
| els | 16,543 | 7,712,358 a | 1,084,136 | 16,511 | 8,136,195 | 1,104,996 | 16,444 | 8,937,103 | 1,150,419 |
| emc | 4,284 a | 5,321,079 a | 1,603,548 a | 4,201 | 5,361,912 a | 1,793,267 a | 1,763 a | 1,120,222 a | 518,777 a |
| feb | 1,856 a | 1,412,281 a | 447,544 a | 1,751 a | 1,198,120 a | 507,656 a | 4,348 a | 7,017,588 a | 2,039,740 a |
| fmc | 59,060 | 67,687,955 | 11,114,804 | 59,343 a | 70,262,626 | 11,651,462 | 66,829 | 78,687,325 | 12,261,465 |
| fum | 43,440 e | NA | NA | 42,918 e | NA | NA | NA | NA | NA |
| ggb | 70,886 a | 24,385,956 a | 1,722,662 a | 70,562 a | 27,763,966 a | 1,832,909 a | 72,326 | 28,093,944 | 1,780,851 |
| lca | See ELCA | See ELCA | See ELCA | See ELCA | See ELCA | See ELCA | See ELCA | See ELCA | See ELCA |
| lms | 1,943,281 | 832,701,255 | 98,139,835 a | 1,951,730 | 855,461,015 | 104,076,876 a | 1,951,391 | 887,928,255 | 110,520,917 |
| mch | 90,139 a | 71,641,773 | 26,832,240 | 90,959 | 76,669,365 | 27,812,549 | 92,161 a | 76,087,609 a | 25,637,872 a |
| mca | 21,409 | 10,996,031 | 1,167,513 | 21,140 | 11,798,536 | 1,237,349 | 21,108 | 12,555,760 | 1,148,478 |
| nab | 43,928 | 37,078,473 | 7,480,331 | 43,744 a | 37,172,560 a | 7,957,860 a | 43,850 | 37,401,175 | 7,986,099 |
| opc | 14,355 | 16,017,003 | 3,376,691 | 15,072 a | 17,883,915 a | 3,467,207 a | 15,072 | 20,090,259 | 3,967,490 |
| pch | 2,665,276 | 1,855,684,719 | 309,978,224 | 2,631,466 | 1,930,179,808 | 322,336,258 | 2,609,191 | 2,064,789,378 | 344,757,186 |
| rca | 183,255 | 164,250,624 | 29,995,068 | 182,342 | 183,975,696 a | 31,271,007 | 180,980 | 181,977,101 a | 32,130,943 a |
| sda | 790,731 | 240,565,576 | 503,334,129 | 809,159 | 242,316,834 | 524,977,061 | 825,654 | 249,591,109 | 552,633,569 |
| sbc | 15,663,296 | 5,209,748,503 | 858,635,435 | 15,691,249 a | 5,987,033,115 | 891,149,403 a | 15,891,514 | 6,098,933,137 | 930,176,909 |
| ucc | 1,472,213 | 578,042,965 | 67,806,448 | 1,452,565 | 615,727,028 | 69,013,791 | 1,438,181 | 651,176,773 | 70,180,193 |
| wel | 314,188 a | 150,853,785 a | 33,193,286 a | 314,379 a | 156,966,741 a | 47,436,904 | 315,355 | 164,256,655 | 52,322,175 |
| Total | 29,791,128 | $12,807,576,187 | $2,461,642,967 | 29,586,894 | $13,388,460,681 | $2,538,962,406 | 29,763,554 | $13,874,600,352 | $2,623,437,318 |

a Data obtained from denominational source.
e Inclusive membership, used only in Chapter 5 analysis.

101

**Appendix B-2: Church Member Giving for 43 Denominations, 1996-1997**

| | Data Year 1996 | | | Data Year 1997 | | |
|---|---|---|---|---|---|---|
| | Full/Confirmed Members | Congregational Finances | Benevolences | Full/Confirmed Members | Congregational Finances | Benevolences |
| Allegheny Wesleyan Methodist Connection (Original Allegheny Conference) | 1,865 | $3,250,449 | $1,127,594 | 1,849 | $3,646,644 | $1,043,494 |
| Apostolic Faith Mission Church of God | 8,500 | 212,000 | 288,000 | 8,100 | 276,000 | 284,000 |
| Christian and Missionary Alliance | 143,157 [a] | 191,479,193 [a] | 38,810,468 [a] | 146,153 | 206,461,968 | 43,022,993 |
| Church of Christ (Holiness) U.S.A. | 10,228 [a] | 7,080,793 [a] | 334,446 [a] | 10,243 | 6,990,146 | 342,400 |
| Church of Lutheran Brethren of America | 8,181 | 8,606,432 | 1,812,818 | 8,232 | 9,459,182 | 1,841,030 |
| Church of the Lutheran Confession | 6,657 | 3,685,658 | 673,511 | 6,510 | 3,821,360 | 650,980 |
| Churches of God General Conference | 31,558 | 17,136,919 | 3,646,977 | 31,557 | 17,204,995 | 3,987,342 |
| The Episcopal Church | 1,593,756 [a] | 1,489,147,691 [a] | 242,580,034 [a] | 1,717,069 [a] | 1,594,945,240 [a] | 237,055,208 [a] |
| International Pentecostal Church of Christ | 2,369 | 2,313,174 | 2,142,620 | 2,494 | 2,472,409 | 2,846,724 |
| Missionary Church, Inc. | 31,548 | 42,282,238 [a] | 7,727,424 [a] | 31,197 | 42,915,770 | 7,938,692 [a] |
| National Association of Free Will Baptists | 210,305 | 57,244,171 [a] | 9,687,919 [a] | 210,305 | 66,900,000 [a] | 14,800,000 [a] |
| Presbyterian Church in America | 218,276 [a] | 271,619,240 [a] | 62,501,779 [a] | 224,855 [a] | 305,924,016 [a] | 70,174,244 [a] |
| United Brethren in Christ, Church of | 24,137 | 20,011,538 | 3,277,564 [a] | 23,585 | 23,770,417 | 3,414,482 |
| The United Methodist Church | 8,496,047 [a] | 2,984,250,917 | 760,441,306 | 8,452,042 [a] | 3,192,213,867 [a] | 798,115,624 [a] |
| The Wesleyan Church | 111,099 | 135,664,782 | 25,945,862 | 111,771 | 148,273,193 | 27,538,109 |

[a]Data obtained from denominational source.

**Appendix B-3.1:   Church Member Giving for Eleven Denominations, 1921-1952, in Current Dollars**

| Year | Total Contributions | Members | Per Capita Giving |
|------|--------------------|---------|--------------------|
| 1921 | $281,173,263 | 17,459,611 | $16.10 |
| 1922 | 345,995,802 | 18,257,426 | 18.95 |
| 1923 | 415,556,876 | 18,866,775 | 22.03 |
| 1924 | 443,187,826 | 19,245,220 | 23.03 |
| 1925 | 412,658,363 | 19,474,863 | 21.19 |
| 1926 | 368,529,223 | 17,054,404 | 21.61 |
| 1927 | 459,527,624 | 20,266,709 | 22.67 |
| 1928 | 429,947,883 | 20,910,584 | 20.56 |
| 1929 | 445,327,233 | 20,612,910 | 21.60 |
| 1930 | 419,697,819 | 20,796,745 | 20.18 |
| 1931 | 367,158,877 | 21,508,745 | 17.07 |
| 1932 | 309,409,873 | 21,757,411 | 14.22 |
| 1933 | 260,366,681 | 21,792,663 | 11.95 |
| 1934 | 260,681,472 | 22,105,624 | 11.79 |
| 1935 | 267,596,925 | 22,204,355 | 12.05 |
| 1936 | 279,835,526 | 21,746,023 | 12.87 |
| 1937 | 297,134,313 | 21,906,456 | 13.56 |
| 1938 | 307,217,666 | 22,330,090 | 13.76 |
| 1939 | 302,300,476 | 23,084,048 | 13.10 |
| 1940 | 311,362,429 | 23,671,660 | 13.15 |
| 1941 | 336,732,622 | 23,120,929 | 14.56 |
| 1942 | 358,419,893 | 23,556,204 | 15.22 |
| 1943 | 400,742,492 | 24,679,784 | 16.24 |
| 1944 | 461,500,396 | 25,217,319 | 18.30 |
| 1945 | 551,404,448 | 25,898,642 | 21.29 |
| 1946 | 608,165,179 | 26,158,559 | 23.25 |
| 1947 | 684,393,895 | 27,082,905 | 25.27 |
| 1948 | 775,360,993 | 27,036,992 | 28.68 |
| 1949 | 875,069,944 | 27,611,824 | 31.69 |
| 1950 | 934,723,015 | 28,176,095 | 33.17 |
| 1951 | 1,033,391,527 | 28,974,314 | 35.67 |
| 1952 | 1,121,802,639 | 29,304,909 | 38.28 |

## Appendix B-3.2: Church Member Giving for Eleven Denominations, 1953-1967

| | Data Year 1953 | | Data Year 1954 | | Data Year 1955 | |
|---|---|---|---|---|---|---|
| | Total Contributions | Per Capita Total Contributions | Total Contributions | Per Capita Total Contributions | Total Contributions | Per Capita Total Contributions |
| American Baptist (Northern) | $66,557,447 a | $44.50 b | $65,354,184 | $43.17 | $67,538,753 d | $44.19 d |
| Christian Church (Disciples of Christ) | 60,065,545 c | 32.50 b | 65,925,164 | 34.77 | 68,611,162 d | 35.96 d |
| Church of the Brethren | 7,458,584 | 43.78 | 7,812,806 | 45.88 | 9,130,616 | 53.00 |
| The Episcopal Church | 84,209,027 | 49.02 | 92,079,668 | 51.84 | 97,541,567 d | 50.94 b |
| Evangelical Lutheran Church in America | | | | | | |
| The American Lutheran Church | | | | | | |
| American Lutheran Church | 30,881,256 | 55.24 | 34,202,987 | 58.83 | 40,411,856 | 67.03 |
| The Evangelical Lutheran Church | 30,313,907 | 48.70 | 33,312,926 | 51.64 | 37,070,341 | 55.29 |
| United Evangelical Lutheran Ch. | 1,953,163 | 55.85 | 2,268,200 | 50.25 | 2,635,469 | 69.84 |
| Lutheran Free Church | Not Reported: YACC 1955, p. 264 | | 2,101,026 | 44.51 | 2,708,747 | 55.76 |
| Evan. Lutheran Churches, Assn. of | Not Reported: YACC 1955, p. 264 | | Not Reported: YACC 1956, p. 276 | | Not Reported: YACC 1957, p. 284 | |
| Lutheran Church in America | | | | | | |
| United Lutheran Church | 67,721,548 | 45.68 | 76,304,344 | 50.25 | 83,170,787 | 53.46 |
| General Council Evang. Luth. Ch. | | | | | | |
| General Synod of Evan. Luth. Ch. | | | | | | |
| United Syn. Evang. Luth. South | | | | | | |
| American Evangelical Luth. Ch. | Not Reported: YACC 1955, p. 264 | | Not Reported: YACC 1956, p. 276 | | Not Reported: YACC 1957, p. 284 | |
| Augustana Lutheran Church | 18,733,019 | 53.98 | 22,203,098 | 62.14 | 22,090,350 | 60.12 |
| Finnish Lutheran Ch. (Suomi Synod) | 744,971 | 32.12 | 674,554 | 29.47 | 1,059,682 | 43.75 |
| Moravian Church in Am. No. Prov. | 1,235,534 | 53.26 | 1,461,658 | 59.51 | 1,241,008 | 49.15 |
| Presbyterian Church (U.S.A.) | | | | | | |
| United Presbyterian Ch. in U.S.A. | | | | | | |
| Presbyterian Church in the U.S.A. | 141,057,179 | 56.49 | 158,110,613 | 61.47 | 180,472,698 | 68.09 |
| United Presbyterian Ch. in N.A. | 13,204,897 | 57.73 | 14,797,353 | 62.37 | 16,019,616 | 65.39 |
| Presbyterian Church in the U.S. | 56,001,996 | 73.99 | 59,222,983 | 75.54 | 66,033,260 | 81.43 |
| Reformed Church in America | 13,671,897 | 68.57 | 14,740,275 | 71.87 | 17,459,572 | 84.05 |
| Southern Baptist Convention | 278,851,129 | 39.84 | 305,573,654 | 42.17 | 334,836,283 | 44.54 |
| United Church of Christ | | | | | | |
| Congregational Christian | 64,061,866 | 49.91 | 71,786,834 | 54.76 | 80,519,810 | 60.00 |
| Congregational | | | | | | |
| Evangelical and Reformed | 31,025,133 | 41.24 | 36,261,267 | 46.83 | 41,363,406 | 52.74 |
| Evangelical Synod of N.A./German | | | | | | |
| Reformed Church in the U.S. | | | | | | |
| The United Methodist Church | | | | | | |
| The Evangelical United Brethren | 36,331,994 | 50.21 | 36,609,598 | 50.43 | 41,199,631 | 56.01 |
| The Methodist Church | 314,521,214 | 34.37 | 345,416,448 | 37.53 | 389,490,613 | 41.82 |
| Methodist Episcopal Church | | | | | | |
| Methodist Episcopal Church South | | | | | | |
| Methodist Protestant Church | | | | | | |
| Total | $1,318,601,306 | | $1,446,219,640 | | $1,600,655,226 | |

a In data year 1953, $805,135 has been subtracted from the 1955 *Yearbook of American Churches* (Edition for 1956) entry. See 1956 *Yearbook of American Churches* (Edition for 1957), p. 276, n.1.

b This Per Capita Total Contributions figure was calculated by dividing (1) revised Total Contributions as listed in this Appendix, by (2) Membership that, for purposes of this report, had been calculated by dividing the unrevised Total Contributions by the Per Capita Total Contributions figures that were published in the *YACC* series.

c In data year 1953, $5,508,883 has been added to the 1955 *Yearbook of American Churches* (Edition for 1956) entry. See 1956 *Yearbook of American Churches* (Edition for 1957), p. 276, n. 4.

d Total Contributions and Per Capita Total Contributions, respectively, prorated based on available data as follows: American Baptist Churches, 1954 and 1957 data; Christian Church (Disciples of Christ), 1954 and 1956 data; and The Episcopal Church, 1954 and 1956 data.

## Appendix B-3.2: Church Member Giving for Eleven Denominations, 1953-1967 (continued)

| | Data Year 1956 | | Data Year 1957 | | Data Year 1958 | |
|---|---|---|---|---|---|---|
| | Total Contributions | Per Capita Total Contributions | Total Contributions | Per Capita Total Contributions | Total Contributions | Per Capita Total Contributions |
| American Baptist (Northern) | $69,723,321 e | $45.21 e | $71,907,890 | $46.23 | $70,405,404 e | $45.03 |
| Christian Church (Disciples of Christ) | 71,397,159 | 37.14 | 73,737,955 | 37.94 | 79,127,458 | 41.17 |
| Church of the Brethren | 10,936,285 | 63.15 | 11,293,388 | 64.43 | 12,288,049 | 70.03 |
| The Episcopal Church | 103,003,465 | 52.79 | 111,660,728 | 53.48 | 120,687,177 | 58.33 |
| Evangelical Lutheran Church in America | | | | | | |
| The American Lutheran Church | 45,316,809 | 72.35 | 44,518,194 | 68.80 | 47,216,896 | 70.89 |
| American Lutheran Church | 39,096,038 | 56.47 | 44,212,046 | 61.95 | 45,366,512 | 61.74 |
| The Evangelical Lutheran Church | 2,843,527 | 73.57 | 2,641,201 | 65.46 | 3,256,050 | 77.38 |
| United Evangelical Lutheran Ch. | 2,652,307 | 53.14 | 3,379,882 | 64.70 | 3,519,017 | 66.31 |
| Lutheran Free Church | Not Reported: YACC 1958, p. 292 | | | | Not Reported: YACC 1960, p. 276 | |
| Evan. Lutheran Churches, Assn. of | | | Not Reported: YACC 1959, p. 277 | | | |
| Lutheran Church in America | | | | | | |
| United Lutheran Church | 93,321,223 | 58.46 | 100,943,860 | 61.89 | 110,179,054 | 66.45 |
| General Council Evang. Luth. Ch. | | | | | | |
| General Synod of Evan. Luth. Ch. | | | | | | |
| United Syn. Evang. Luth. South | | | | | | |
| American Evangelical Luth. Ch. | Not Comparable YACC 1958, p. 292 | | 935,319 | 59.45 | 1,167,503 | 72.98 |
| Augustana Lutheran Church | 24,893,792 | 66.15 | 28,180,152 | 72.09 | 29,163,771 | 73.17 |
| Finnish Lutheran Ch. (Suomi Synod) | 1,308,026 | 51.56 | 1,524,299 | 58.11 | 1,533,058 | 61.94 |
| Moravian Church in Am. No. Prov. | 1,740,961 | 67.53 | 1,776,703 | 67.77 | 1,816,281 | 68.14 |
| Presbyterian Church (U.S.A.) | | | | | | |
| United Presbyterian Ch. in U.S.A. | 204,208,085 | 75.02 | 214,253,598 | 77.06 | 243,000,572 | 78.29 |
| Presbyterian Church in the U.S.A. | 18,424,936 | 73.30 | 19,117,837 | 74.24 | | |
| United Presbyterian Ch. in N.A. | | | | | | |
| Presbyterian Church in the U.S. | 73,477,555 | 88.56 | 78,426,424 | 92.03 | 82,760,291 | 95.18 |
| Reformed Church in America | 18,718,008 | 88.56 | 19,658,604 | 91.10 | 21,550,017 | 98.24 |
| Southern Baptist Convention | 372,136,675 | 48.17 | 397,540,347 | 49.99 | 419,619,438 | 51.04 |
| United Church of Christ | | | | | | |
| Congregational Christian | 89,914,505 | 65.18 | 90,333,453 | 64.87 | 97,480,446 | 69.55 |
| Congregational | | | | | | |
| Evangelical and Reformed | 51,519,531 | 64.88 | 55,718,141 | 69.56 | 63,419,468 | 78.56 |
| Evangelical Synod of N.A/German | | | | | | |
| Reformed Church in the U.S. | | | | | | |
| The United Methodist Church | | | | | | |
| The Evangelical United Brethren | 44,727,060 | 60.57 | 45,738,332 e | 61.75 e | 46,749,605 e | 62.93 e |
| The Methodist Church | 413,893,955 | 43.82 | 462,826,269 e | 48.31 e | 511,758,582 | 52.80 |
| Methodist Episcopal Church | | | | | | |
| Methodist Episcopal Church South | | | | | | |
| Methodist Protestant Church | | | | | | |
| Total | $1,753,253,223 | | $1,880,324,622 | | $2,012,064,649 | |

e Total Contributions and Per Capita Total Contributions, respectively, prorated based on available data as follows: American Baptist Churches, 1954 and 1957 data; The Evangelical United Brethren, 1956 and 1960 data; and The Methodist Church, 1956 and 1958 data.

## Appendix B-3.2: Church Member Giving for Eleven Denominations, 1953-1967 (continued)

| | Data Year 1959 | | Data Year 1960 | | Data Year 1961 | |
|---|---|---|---|---|---|---|
| | Total Contributions | Per Capita Total Contributions | Total Contributions | Per Capita Total Contributions | Total Contributions | Per Capita Total Contributions |
| American Baptist (Northern) | $74,877,669 | $48.52 | $73,106,232 | $48.06 | $104,887,025 | $68.96 |
| Christian Church (Disciples of Christ) | 84,375,152 f | 51.22 | 86,834,944 | 63.26 | 89,730,589 | 65.31 |
| Church of the Brethren | 12,143,983 | 65.27 | 12,644,194 | 68.33 | 13,653,155 | 73.33 |
| The Episcopal Church | 130,279,752 | 61.36 | 140,625,284 | 64.51 | 154,458,809 | 68.30 |
| Evangelical Lutheran Church in America | | | | | | |
| The American Lutheran Church | 50,163,078 | 73.52 | 51,898,875 | 74.49 | 113,645,260 | 73.28 |
| The Evangelical Lutheran Church | 49,488,063 | 65.56 | 51,297,348 | 66.85 | | |
| United Evangelical Lutheran Ch. | Not Reported: YACC 1961, p. 273 | | Not Reported: YACC 1963, p. 273 | | | |
| Lutheran Free Church | 3,354,270 | 61.20 | 3,618,418 | 63.98 | 4,316,925 | 73.46 |
| Evan. Lutheran Churches, Assn. of | Not Reported: YACC 1961, p. 273 | | Not Reported: YACC 1963, p. 273 | | | |
| Lutheran Church in America | | | | | | |
| United Lutheran Church | 114,458,260 | 68.29 | 119,447,895 | 70.86 | 128,850,845 | 76.18 |
| General Council Evang. Luth. Ch. | | | | | | |
| General Synod of Evan. Luth. Ch. | | | | | | |
| United Syn. Evang. Luth. South | | | | | | |
| American Evangelical Luth. Ch. | 1,033,907 | 63.83 | 1,371,600 | 83.63 | 1,209,752 | 74.89 |
| Augustana Lutheran Church | 31,279,335 | 76.97 | 33,478,865 | 80.88 | 37,863,105 | 89.37 |
| Finnish Lutheran Ch. (Suomi Synod) | 1,685,342 | 68.61 | 1,860,481 | 76.32 | 1,744,550 | 70.60 |
| Moravian Church in Am. No. Prov. | 2,398,565 | 89.28 | 2,252,536 | 82.95 | 2,489,930 | 90.84 |
| Presbyterian Church (U.S.A.) | | | | | | |
| United Presbyterian Ch. in U.S.A. | 259,679,057 | 82.30 | 270,233,943 | 84.31 | 285,380,476 | 87.90 |
| Presbyterian Church in the U.S.A. | | | | | | |
| United Presbyterian Ch. in N.A. | | | | | | |
| Presbyterian Church in the U.S. | 88,404,631 | 99.42 | 91,582,428 | 101.44 | 96,637,354 | 105.33 |
| Reformed Church in America | 22,970,935 | 103.23 | 23,615,749 | 104.53 | 25,045,773 | 108.80 |
| Southern Baptist Convention | 453,338,720 | 53.88 | 480,608,972 | 55.68 | 501,301,714 | 50.24 |
| United Church of Christ | | | | | | |
| Congregational Christian | 100,938,267 | 71.12 | 104,862,037 | 73.20 | 105,871,158 | 73.72 |
| Congregational | | | | | | |
| Evangelical and Reformed | 65,541,874 | 80.92 | 62,346,084 | 76.58 | 65,704,662 | 80.33 |
| Evangelical Synod of N.A./German | | | | | | |
| Reformed Church in the U.S. | | | | | | |
| The United Methodist Church | | | | | | |
| The Evangelical United Brethren | 47,760,877 g | 64.10 g | 48,772,149 | 65.28 | 50,818,912 | 68.12 |
| The Methodist Church | 532,854,842 g | 53.97 g | 553,951,102 | 55.14 | 581,504,618 | 57.27 |
| Methodist Episcopal Church | | | | | | |
| Methodist Episcopal Church South | | | | | | |
| Methodist Protestant Church | | | | | | |
| **Total** | $2,127,026,579 | | $2,214,409,136 | | $2,365,114,612 | |

f The 1961 YACC, p. 273 indicates that data for this year is not comparable with data for the previous year.
g Total Contributions and Per Capita Total Contributions, respectively, prorated based on available data as follows: The Evangelical United Brethren, 1956 and 1960 data; and The Methodist Church, 1958 and 1960 data.

# Appendix B-3.2: Church Member Giving for Eleven Denominations, 1953-1967 (continued)

| | Data Year 1962 | | Data Year 1963 | | Data Year 1964 | |
|---|---|---|---|---|---|---|
| | Total Contributions | Per Capita Total Contributions | Total Contributions | Per Capita Total Contributions | Total Contributions | Per Capita Total Contributions |
| American Baptist (Northern) | $105,667,332 | $68.42 | $99,001,651 | $68.34 | $104,699,557 | $69.99 |
| Christian Church (Disciples of Christ) | 91,889,457 | 67.20 | 96,607,038 | 75.81 | 102,102,840 | 86.44 |
| Church of the Brethren | 14,594,572 | 77.88 | 14,574,688 | 72.06 | 15,221,162 | 76.08 |
| The Episcopal Church | 155,971,264 | 69.80 | 171,125,464 | 76.20 | 175,374,777 | 76.66 |
| Evangelical Lutheran Church in America | | | | | | |
| The American Lutheran Church | 114,912,112 | 72.47 | 136,202,292 | 81.11 | 143,687,165 | 83.83 |
| American Lutheran Church | | | | | | |
| The Evangelical Lutheran Church | | | | | | |
| United Evangelical Lutheran Ch. | | | | | | |
| Lutheran Free Church | 4,765,138 | 78.68 | | | | |
| Evan. Lutheran Churches, Assn. of | | | | | | |
| Lutheran Church in America | 185,166,857 | 84.98 | 157,423,391 | 71.45 | 170,012,096 | 76.35 |
| United Lutheran Church | | | | | | |
| General Council Evang. Luth. Ch. | | | | | | |
| General Synod of Evan. Luth. Ch. | | | | | | |
| United Syn. Evang. Luth. South | | | | | | |
| American Evangelical Luth. Ch. | | | | | | |
| Augustana Lutheran Church | | | | | | |
| Finnish Lutheran Ch. (Suomi Synod) | | | | | | |
| Moravian Church in Am. No. Prov. | 2,512,133 | 91.92 | 2,472,273 | 89.29 | 2,868,694 | 103.54 |
| Presbyterian Church (U.S.A.) | | | | | | |
| United Presbyterian Ch. in U.S.A. | 288,496,652 | 88.08 | 297,582,313 | 90.46 | 304,833,435 | 92.29 |
| Presbyterian Church in the U.S.A. | | | | | | |
| United Presbyterian Ch. in N.A. | | | | | | |
| Presbyterian Church in the U.S. | 99,262,431 | 106.96 | 102,625,764 | 109.46 | 108,269,579 | 114.61 |
| Reformed Church in America | 25,579,443 | 110.16 | 26,918,484 | 117.58 | 29,174,103 | 126.44 |
| Southern Baptist Convention | 540,811,457 | 53.06 | 556,042,694 | 53.49 | 591,587,981 | 55.80 |
| United Church of Christ | 164,858,968 | 72.83 | 162,379,019 | 73.12 | 169,208,042 | 75.94 |
| Congregational Christian | | | | | | |
| Congregational | | | | | | |
| Evangelical and Reformed | | | | | | |
| Evangelical Synod of N.A./German | | | | | | |
| Reformed Church in the U.S. | | | | | | |
| The United Methodist Church | | | | | | |
| The Evangelical United Brethren | 54,567,962 | 72.91 | 49,921,568 | 67.37 | 56,552,783 | 76.34 |
| The Methodist Church | 599,081,561 | 58.53 | 613,547,721 | 59.60 | 608,841,881 | 59.09 |
| Methodist Episcopal Church | | | | | | |
| Methodist Episcopal Church South | | | | | | |
| Methodist Protestant Church | | | | | | |
| Total | $2,448,137,339 | | $2,486,424,360 | | $2,582,434,095 | |

Note: Data for the years 1965 through 1967 was not available in a form that could be readily analyzed for the present purposes, and therefore data for 1965-1967 was estimated as described in the introductory comments to Appendix B. See Appendix B-1 for 1968-1991 data except for The Episcopal Church and The United Methodist Church, available data for which is presented in the continuation of Appendix B-3 in the table immediately following.

## Appendix B-3.3: Church Member Giving for Eleven Denominations, The Episcopal Church and The United Methodist Church, 1968-1997

| The Episcopal Church | | | | The United Methodist Church | | |
|---|---|---|---|---|---|---|
| Data Year | Total Contributions | Full/Confirmed Membership | | Data Year | Total Contributions | Full/Confirmed Membership |
| 1968 | $202,658,092 c | 2,322,911 c | | 1968 | $763,000,434 a | 10,849,375 b |
| 1969 | 209,989,189 c | 2,238,538 | | 1969 | 800,425,000 | 10,671,774 |
| 1970 | 248,702,969 | 2,208,773 | | 1970 | 819,945,000 | 10,509,198 |
| 1971 | 257,523,469 | 2,143,557 | | 1971 | 843,103,000 | 10,334,521 |
| 1972 | 270,245,645 | 2,099,896 | | 1972 | 885,708,000 | 10,192,265 |
| 1973 | 296,735,919 c | 2,079,873 c | | 1973 | 935,723,000 | 10,063,046 |
| 1974 | 305,628,925 | 2,069,793 | | 1974 | 1,009,760,804 | 9,957,710 |
| 1975 | 352,243,222 | 2,051,914 c | | 1975 | 1,081,080,372 | 9,861,028 |
| 1976 | 375,942,065 | 2,021,057 | | 1976 | 1,162,828,991 | 9,785,534 |
| 1977 | 401,814,395 | 2,114,638 | | 1977 | 1,264,191,548 | 9,731,779 |
| 1978 | 430,116,564 | 1,975,234 | | 1978 | 1,364,460,266 | 9,653,711 |
| 1979 | 484,211,412 | 1,962,062 | | 1979 | 1,483,481,986 | 9,584,771 |
| 1980 | 507,315,457 | 1,933,080 c | | 1980 | 1,632,204,336 | 9,519,407 |
| 1981 | 697,816,298 | 1,930,690 | | 1981 | 1,794,706,741 | 9,457,012 |
| 1982 | 778,184,068 | 1,922,923 c | | 1982 | 1,931,796,533 | 9,405,164 |
| 1983 | 876,844,252 | 1,906,618 | | 1983 | 2,049,437,917 | 9,291,936 |
| 1984 | 939,796,743 | 1,896,056 | | 1984 | 2,211,306,198 | 9,266,853 |
| 1985 | 1,043,117,983 | 1,881,250 | | 1985 | 2,333,928,274 | 9,192,172 |
| 1986 | 1,134,455,479 | 1,772,271 c | | 1986 | 2,460,079,431 | 9,124,575 |
| 1987 | 1,181,378,441 | 1,741,036 | | 1987 | 2,573,748,234 | 9,055,145 |
| 1988 | 1,209,378,098 | 1,725,581 | | 1988 | 2,697,918,285 | 8,979,139 |
| 1989 | 1,309,243,747 | 1,714,122 | | 1989 | 2,845,998,177 | 8,904,824 |
| 1990 | 1,377,794,610 | 1,698,240 | | 1990 | 2,967,535,538 | 8,853,455 |
| 1991 | 1,541,141,356 c | 1,613,825 c | | 1991 | 3,099,522,282 | 8,789,101 |
| 1992 | 1,582,055,527 c | 1,615,930 c | | 1992 | 3,202,700,721 c | 8,726,951 c |
| 1993 | 1,617,623,255 c | 1,580,339 c | | 1993 | 3,303,255,279 | 8,646,595 |
| 1994 | 1,679,250,095 c | 1,578,282 c | | 1994 | 3,430,351,778 | 8,584,125 |
| 1995 | 1,840,431,636 c | 1,584,225 c | | 1995 | 3,568,359,334 c | 8,538,808 c |
| 1996 | 1,731,727,725 c | 1,593,756 c | | 1996 | 3,744,692,223 | 8,496,047 c |
| 1997 | 1,832,000,448 c | 1,717,069 c | | 1997 | 3,990,329,491 c | 8,452,042 c |

[a] The Evangelical United Brethren Data Not Reported: *YACC* 1970, p. 198-200. This figure is the sum of The Methodist Church in 1968, and the Evangelical United Brethren data for 1967.
[b] This membership figure is an average of the sum of 1967 membership for The Methodist Church and the Evangelical United Brethren and 1969 data for The United Methodist Church.
[c] Data obtained directly from denominational source.
Note: Data in italics indicates a change from the previous edition in the series.

# APPENDIX B-4: *Trends in Giving and Membership*

## Appendix B-4.1: Membership for Seven Denominations, 1968-1997

| Year | American Baptist Churches (Total Mem.) | Assemblies of God | Baptist General Conference | Christian and Missionary Alliance | Church of God (Cleveland, TN) | Roman Catholic Church | Salvation Army |
|---|---|---|---|---|---|---|---|
| 1968 | 1,583,560 | 610,946 | 100,000 | 71,656 | 243,532 | 47,468,333 | 329,515 |
| 1969 | 1,528,019 | 626,660 | 101,226 | 70,573 | 257,995 | 47,872,089 | 331,711 |
| 1970 | 1,472,478 | 625,027 | 103,955 | 71,708 | 272,276 | 48,214,729 | 326,934 |
| 1971 | 1,562,636 | 645,891 | 108,474 | 73,547 | 287,099 | 48,390,990 | 335,684 |
| 1972 | 1,484,393 | 679,813 | 111,364 | 77,991 | 297,103 | 48,460,427 | 358,626 |
| 1973 | 1,502,759 | 700,071 | 109,033 | 77,606 | 313,332 | 48,465,438 | 361,571 |
| 1974 | 1,579,029 | 751,818 | 111,093 | 80,412 | 328,892 | 48,701,835 | 366,471 |
| 1975 | 1,603,033 | 785,348 | 115,340 | 83,628 | 343,249 | 48,881,872 | 384,817 |
| 1976 | 1,593,574 | 898,711 | 117,973 | 83,978 | 365,124 | 49,325,752 | 380,618 |
| 1977 | 1,584,517 | 939,312 | 120,222 | 88,763 | 377,765 | 49,836,176 | 396,238 |
| 1978 | 1,589,610 | 932,365 | 131,000 | 88,903 | 392,551 | 49,602,035 | 414,035 |
| 1979 | 1,600,521 | 958,418 | 126,800 | 96,324 | 441,385 | 49,812,178 | 414,659 |
| 1980 | 1,607,541 | 1,064,490 | 133,385 | 106,050 | 435,012 | 50,449,842 | 417,359 |
| 1981 | 1,621,795 | 1,103,134 | 127,662 | 109,558 | 456,797 | 51,207,579 | 414,999 |
| 1982 | 1,637,099 | 1,119,686 | 129,928 | 112,745 | 463,992 | 52,088,774 | 419,475 |
| 1983 | 1,620,153 | 1,153,935 | 131,594 | 117,501 | 493,904 | 52,392,934 | 428,046 |
| 1984 | 1,559,683 | 1,189,143 | 131,162 | 120,250 | 505,775 | 52,286,043 | 420,971 |
| 1985 | 1,576,483 | 1,235,403 | 130,193 | 123,602 | 521,061 | 52,654,908 | 427,825 |
| 1986 | 1,568,778 | 1,258,724 | 132,546 | 130,116 | 536,346 | 52,893,217 | 432,893 |
| 1987 | 1,561,656 | 1,275,146 | 136,688 | 131,354 | 551,632 | 53,496,862 | 434,002 |
| 1988 | 1,548,573 | 1,275,148 | 134,396 | 133,575 | 556,917 | 54,918,949 | 433,448 |
| 1989 | 1,535,971 | 1,266,982 | 135,125 | 134,336 | 582,203 | 57,019,948 | 445,566 |
| 1990 | 1,527,840 | 1,298,121 | 133,742 | 138,071 | 620,393 | 58,568,015 | 445,991 |
| 1991 | 1,534,078 | 1,324,800 | 134,717 | 141,077 | 646,201 | 58,267,424 | 446,403 |
| 1992 | 1,538,710 | 1,337,321 | 134,658 | 142,346 | 672,008 | 59,220,723 | 450,028 |
| 1993 | 1,516,505 | 1,340,400 | 134,814 | 147,367 | 700,517 | 59,858,042 | 450,312 |
| 1994 | 1,507,934 | 1,354,337 | 135,128 | 147,560 | 722,541 | 60,190,605 | 443,246 |
| 1995 | 1,517,400 | 1,377,320 | 135,008 | 147,955 | 753,230 | 60,280,454 | 453,150 |
| 1996 | 1,503,267 | 1,407,941 | 136,120 | 143,157 | 773,483 | 61,207,914 | 462,744 |
| 1997 | 1,478,534 | 1,419,717 | 134,795 | 146,153 | 815,042 | 61,563,769 | 468,262 |

Note regarding American Baptist Churches in the U.S.A. Total Membership data: Total Membership is used for the American Baptist Churches in the U.S.A. for analyses that consider membership as a percentage of U.S. population. The ABC denominational office is the source for this data in the years 1968 and from 1986 through 1992. The year 1969 is an average of the years 1968 and 1970. The year 1978 Total Membership data figure is an adjustment of *YACC* data based on 1981 *YACC* information.

# APPENDIX C: *Income, Deflators, and U.S. Population*

Appendix C.1 presents U.S. Per Capita Disposable Personal Income for 1921 through 1997.

The Implicit Price Index for Gross National Product is provided for 1921 through 1996. The series keyed to 1992 dollars provided deflators only from 1929 through 1997. Therefore, the 1921 through 1928 data was converted to inflation-adjusted 1958 dollars using the series keyed to 1958=100, and the inflation-adjusted 1958 dollar values were then converted to inflation-adjusted 1992 dollars using the series keyed to 1992 dollars.

Appendix C.2 presents U.S. population for 1921 through 1997.

**SOURCES**
**Income 1921-1928, Deflator 1921-1928, and U.S. Population, 1921-1928**
*Historical Statistics of the United States: Colonial Times to 1970 Bicentennial Edition, Part 1* (Washington, DC: Bureau of the Census, 1975):
  1921-28 Per Capita Disposable Personal Income: Series F 9, p. 224 (F 6-9).
  1921-28 Implicit Price Index GNP (1958=100): Series F 9, p. 224 (F 6-9).
  1921-28 U.S. population: Series A-7, p. 8 (A6-8).
**Income 1929-1981**

  Per Capita Disposable Personal Income in Current Dollars: U.S. Department of Commerce, Bureau of Economic Analysis, National Income and Product Accounts of the United States, 1929-94, Volume 2. Washington, DC: U.S. Government Printing Office, 1998, Table 8.3, p. 306.

**Income 1982-94**

  Per Capita Disposable Personal Income in Current Dollars: U.S. Department of Commerce, Bureau of Economic Analysis, *Survey of Current Business*, August 1998, Table 2.1, p. 128.

**Income 1995-97**

  Per Capita Disposable Personal Income in Current Dollars: U.S. Department of Commerce, Bureau of Economic Analysis, *Survey of Current Business*, August 1998, Table 8.2, p. 109. 1997 also in *SCB*, August 1999, Table 2.1, p. D-6.
**Deflator in 1992 Dollars, 1929-1997**

  Gross National Product: Implicit Price Deflators for Gross National Product: U.S. Bureau of Economic Analysis, *Survey of Current Business*, August 1998, Table 3, p. 159. 1997 also in *SCB*, August 1999, Table 7.3, p. D-18.
**U.S. Population 1929-1958**

  U.S. Population: U.S. Department of Commerce, Bureau of Economic Analysis, National Income and Product Accounts of the United States: Vol. 1, 1929-58, February 1993, Table 8.2, p. 190.

**U.S. Population 1959-88**

  U.S. Population: U.S. Department of Commerce, Bureau of Economic Analysis, National Income and Product Accounts of the United States: Vol. 2, 1959-88, September 1992, Table 8.2, p. 330.

**U.S. Population 1989-97**

  U.S. Population: U.S. Department of Commerce, Bureau of Economic Analysis, *Survey of Current Business*
    **1989:** December 1991, p. 16.
    **1990-93:** July 1994, p. 111.
    **1994:** July 1996, p. 27.
    **1995:** May 1997, p. D-25.
    **1996:** July 1998, Table 8.3, p. D-25.
    **1997:** August 1999, Table 8.3, p. D-25

## Appendix C: Per Capita Disposable Personal Income and Deflators, 1921-1997

| Year | Current $s Per Capita Disposable Personal Income | Implicit Price Deflator GNP [1958= 100] | Implicit Price Deflator GNP [1992= 100] | Year | Current $s Per Capita Disposable Personal Income | Implicit Price Deflator GNP [1992= 100] |
|------|------|------|------|------|------|------|
| 1921 | $555 | 54.5 | | 1960 | $2,013 | 23.28 |
| 1922 | 548 | 50.1 | | 1961 | 2,066 | 23.55 |
| 1923 | 623 | 51.3 | | 1962 | 2,156 | 23.85 |
| 1924 | 626 | 51.2 | | 1963 | 2,229 | 24.13 |
| 1925 | 630 | 51.9 | | 1964 | 2,389 | 24.49 |
| 1926 | 659 | 51.1 | | 1965 | 2,546 | 24.97 |
| 1927 | 650 | 50.0 | | 1966 | 2,720 | 25.68 |
| 1928 | 643 | 50.8 | | 1967 | 2,882 | 26.50 |
| 1929 | 680 | | 13.12 | 1968 | 3,101 | 27.66 |
| 1930 | 602 | | 12.65 | 1969 | 3,302 | 28.96 |
| 1931 | 515 | | 11.34 | 1970 | 3,550 | 30.50 |
| 1932 | 390 | | 10.02 | 1971 | 3,811 | 32.08 |
| 1933 | 363 | | 9.74 | 1972 | 4,082 | 33.44 |
| 1934 | 414 | | 10.28 | 1973 | 4,562 | 35.32 |
| 1935 | 461 | | 10.47 | 1974 | 4,941 | 38.49 |
| 1936 | 520 | | 10.59 | 1975 | 5,383 | 42.11 |
| 1937 | 554 | | 11.04 | 1976 | 5,856 | 44.58 |
| 1938 | 506 | | 10.72 | 1977 | 6,383 | 47.46 |
| 1939 | 539 | | 10.61 | 1978 | 7,123 | 50.92 |
| 1940 | 575 | | 10.76 | 1979 | 7,888 | 55.26 |
| 1941 | 697 | | 11.50 | 1980 | 8,697 | 60.36 |
| 1942 | 872 | | 12.35 | 1981 | 9,601 | 66.05 |
| 1943 | 982 | | 13.02 | 1982 | 10,132 | 70.21 |
| 1944 | 1,062 | | 13.36 | 1983 | 10,776 | 73.20 |
| 1945 | 1,077 | | 13.72 | 1984 | 11,912 | 75.97 |
| 1946 | 1,136 | | 15.38 | 1985 | 12,592 | 78.57 |
| 1947 | 1,185 | | 17.10 | 1986 | 13,211 | 80.62 |
| 1948 | 1,297 | | 18.10 | 1987 | 13,851 | 83.09 |
| 1949 | 1,272 | | 18.10 | 1988 | 14,881 | 86.12 |
| 1950 | 1,382 | | 18.29 | 1989 | 15,771 | 89.75 |
| 1951 | 1,492 | | 19.60 | 1990 | 16,689 | 93.63 |
| 1952 | 1,545 | | 19.94 | 1991 | 17,179 | 97.33 |
| 1953 | 1,617 | | 20.19 | 1992 | 18,029 | 100.00 |
| 1954 | 1,625 | | 20.41 | 1993 | 18,558 | 102.63 |
| 1955 | 1,710 | | 20.75 | 1994 | 19,251 | 105.08 |
| 1956 | 1,794 | | 21.47 | 1995 | 20,050 | 107.49 |
| 1957 | 1,859 | | 22.18 | 1996 | 20,840 | 109.50 |
| 1958 | 1,892 | | 22.72 | 1997 | 21,633 | 111.52 |
| 1959 | 1,975 | | 22.96 | | | |

## Appendix C.2: U.S. Population, 1921-1997

| Year | U.S. Population | Year | U.S. Population |
|------|-----------------|------|-----------------|
| 1921 | 108,538,000 | 1960 | 180,760,000 |
| 1922 | 110,049,000 | 1961 | 183,742,000 |
| 1923 | 111,947,000 | 1962 | 186,590,000 |
| 1924 | 114,109,000 | 1963 | 189,300,000 |
| 1925 | 115,829,000 | 1964 | 191,927,000 |
| 1926 | 117,397,000 | 1965 | 194,347,000 |
| 1927 | 119,035,000 | 1966 | 196,599,000 |
| 1928 | 120,509,000 | 1967 | 198,752,000 |
| 1929 | 121,878,000 | 1968 | 200,745,000 |
| 1930 | 123,188,000 | 1969 | 202,736,000 |
| 1931 | 124,149,000 | 1970 | 205,089,000 |
| 1932 | 124,949,000 | 1971 | 207,692,000 |
| 1933 | 125,690,000 | 1972 | 209,924,000 |
| 1934 | 126,485,000 | 1973 | 211,939,000 |
| 1935 | 127,362,000 | 1974 | 213,898,000 |
| 1936 | 128,181,000 | 1975 | 215,981,000 |
| 1937 | 128,961,000 | 1976 | 218,086,000 |
| 1938 | 129,969,000 | 1977 | 220,289,000 |
| 1939 | 131,028,000 | 1978 | 222,629,000 |
| 1940 | 132,122,000 | 1979 | 225,106,000 |
| 1941 | 133,402,000 | 1980 | 227,715,000 |
| 1942 | 134,860,000 | 1981 | 229,989,000 |
| 1943 | 136,739,000 | 1982 | 232,201,000 |
| 1944 | 138,397,000 | 1983 | 234,326,000 |
| 1945 | 139,928,000 | 1984 | 236,393,000 |
| 1946 | 141,389,000 | 1985 | 238,510,000 |
| 1947 | 144,126,000 | 1986 | 240,691,000 |
| 1948 | 146,631,000 | 1987 | 242,860,000 |
| 1949 | 149,188,000 | 1988 | 245,093,000 |
| 1950 | 151,684,000 | 1989 | 247,405,000 |
| 1951 | 154,287,000 | 1990 | 249,951,000 |
| 1952 | 156,954,000 | 1991 | 252,688,000 |
| 1953 | 159,565,000 | 1992 | 255,484,000 |
| 1954 | 162,391,000 | 1993 | 258,290,000 |
| 1955 | 165,275,000 | 1994 | 260,681,000 |
| 1956 | 168,221,000 | 1995 | 263,090,000 |
| 1957 | 171,274,000 | 1996 | 265,579,000 |
| 1958 | 174,141,000 | 1997 | 267,880,000 |
| 1959 | 177,073,000 |  |  |